You Can't Take Your Credit Card With You When You Go...

The Moment of Truth ~ Oneness
BOOK II

Anna Coffer

authorHOUSE®

AuthorHouse™
1663 Liberty Drive
Bloomington, IN 47403
www.authorhouse.com
Phone: 1-800-839-8640

Published by AuthorHouse 1/10/2013

ISBN: 978-1-4772-9939-5 (sc)

Any people depicted in stock imagery provided by Thinkstock are models, and such images are being used for illustrative purposes only. Certain stock imagery © Thinkstock.

This book is printed on acid-free paper.

Because of the dynamic nature of the Internet, any web addresses or links contained in this book may have changed since publication and may no longer be valid.

The views expressed in this work are solely those of the author and do not necessarily reflect the views of the publisher, and the publisher hereby disclaims any responsibility for them.

Peace within a tree

I breeze within the windy soul
of forever and tomorrow,
sightless seeing cause of much
but bright lights never borrow

'cause love's not bent on shame nor pride
instinctively wiser still,
comfort of love's own hand
in life's time until

the Sun is never one or two
but seven, six or three.
No battle in One, no fight to win
I'm peace within a tree.

Feel my branches not in sorrow
wiser than the moon.
No chaff or mellow drama left
to bring down life too soon.

Peace as me
peace as you,
peace in One
war eschew

so deep within that angels sing
to tell of your new inner state,
blooming consciousness of mystic love
hate no more this plate

of consciousness and beam bright
with wisdom, joy and merry light.
Say, "I love me and life's delight!"
And math the magic, beam bright light!

Do the math, don't bereft
causal of delight and sing.
Best of all be good to people,
least their heart not bring

wonder dust and life's good
of heaven from above,
'cause a heart can be broken in two
if left unkempt, unloved.

Table of Contents

Acknowledgments

I would like to thank my parents Perfecto Bennie and Jimmieteena Berlita Estorel for tolerating my insistent nature to play in otter-likeness to the alarm of even my three grown-up children to insist the *aliveness* of playfulness must have meaning at some point in existence. Anywhere by this point would be nice.

I knew the rules of existence. When young I hurried through any assignment be it of school or work chores to get to the meaning of life, joy itself with its playfulness. I understood not a world out of harmony with its unrelenting emphasis compounding *all work and no play* to stand toe to toe with wisdom to be aligned first to be clothed with humility to ascribe to its wisdom of our work's need to balance a season of play. Some fear me too playful with its instance to innocent myself as love would have me. "Play at all cost!" became a mantra of wisdom I accrued myself within so love have me whole. Playfulness our season, then.

Taking out time alike to play attires one within in innocence as anyone meaning to keep to the principal where love matters. It was us that confounded life to no end ~ for what baby the entire planet over could survive a hostile area as ours?

Just be aware we do that.

I would too like to thank also Eckhart Tolle for his insistence we peace our planet.

I would like to mention likewise Carol Castello of the San Antonio Eckhart Tolle meet-up group for insisting I put what I was saying to her on paper for if not for her encouraging word at that precise time to be insistent a message of love, I would have given up on the thought that the world over we could all be One again.

"Impossible feat!" I said for I witnessed so little response to One ourselves. What to do for our lovelessness for the other? I felt defeated at every turn. So thank you Carol. You were that one friend I was so in need of.

Love humanity, any takers?

Introduction

Many people are to be thanked for the book itself was inspired to help those that were in need of love today, myself included. I would like to thank the clouds mainly for her patience with humanity and for absorbing all the indifference we have heaped upon her, ourselves and in our societies the world over. "You Can't Take Your Credit Card With You When You Go" is about us as a species loving itself or just another way to say 'a return to love as us'. I welcome you to embrace the inevitable ~ our soul as One among mankind including and not withstanding our ability to trust the other with the most precious gift we have to offer another, our love.

Love within peace

Everyone loves a
happy
ending.
Beginnings are
endings
unknowable
to us.
See how wise it is for us
to be true
to our soul's forgetful nature.

Oneness of being

Who of us is in need of love?

Every now and then a book comes along to excite and profound the reader. This is such a situation. No other book has done what this book will do. There are secrets revealed so untold yet true. Wisdom has a name ~ us, as the being within our humanity.

As a corridor can be hidden and in secret ~ it's fun when we chance an elusive moment to unsecret itself, too. Our mind is such an essence for though the common person phantoms little of its workings, here again the truth be told at least given as a tone any and every part of the mind nor its secrets are unseen as any puzzlement set before the human brain though unknowable is already in existence and therefore knowable, at least to me.

Let's begin then…peace is *Us* as One.

The puzzle of life is not new yet answerable. Wisdom has merits. Secrets phantom our existence. Unknowable wealth, unseeable wave-lengths to carry our existence into any or all existences foreign, foe or friend expedience's '*within*'.

Spiritual teacher Eckhart Tolle has spoken of going '*within*' to find the light of consciousness, our awakening on the matter of our Oneness, so here goes for the sake of being enlightened. I'm doing just that for wisdom to stay its presence. Let's carefully examine our existence together and land who-knows-where when we return, for time and again I will pull you into 'spaceless above' where only love can conform to our ability to access the One as to bring *it* through a form called 'me.'

Constant fear and doubt is construed okay by the norm. Since this issue the world over is being read as I speak, let's get into the issue for the sake of convenience. Love its premise. Don't laugh. Seems every other theme be it reading material, movie or any situation ~ love is the must that everyone at least knows (and I say that lightly) is suppose to be happening. (My side is hurting) ...but touch on the condition of us as a human race gone amuck on a premise so pure and light its substance, that I'd be wrong not to point out an area or two that counts as being of love, yet... (my heart hurts here) due to the human nature of our soul, we've gravitated in such unloving an area that to miss it would be impossible. Keeping us on track with peace is the issue.

Humanity is so lost without a loving existence. Please take note that humanity is responsible to love. Peace is so far removed from our grasp at present the next best thing is to get moving to helping out, least everything in existence bow in defiance to love and for once we will have to decipher that the will of the One 'us' being a part of that endeavor gets what's going to transpire as a loveless existence if and until we do our part. Is this the message of the century? You better believe it is! Without the cooperation of humanity, no love as 'Is'.

There is no way love will exist unless we do our part. So many songs have been written about us negating our part, so many people know the truth. The wisdom of the truth goes without saying, "Please, cast a stone away from your own shadow self."

What will happen as each member in society takes its place as a loving being? Let's say for the sake of the illusion that will take place because what is it to blind society steeped in its own knowledge to listen to wisdom?

People like being smart. Everybody has their share of it for without intelligence we as a society could not function. Every person is loved whether they understand the principal of love or not. Higher wisdom dictates we do the same to ourselves as we would have another do unto our soul, preferably be sweet and kind to us.

When someone says, "Hey stupid or you're dumb or hey chubby," why is that not being a good neighbor? A bird flies without ever knowing of its higher wisdom or the existence of higher power within. That is true of most who have been enlightened. Consciousness just 'is'. It is and will be infinite.

As love will accrue to anyone needing of its help and helper in spirit as formless 'One,' then let us partake of it. Love is never absent, it's present always. To be absent of love can happen, though. I'm sure some of you smarting over an incident where love didn't transpire will agree with me here.

When someone is amazed at the teaching of a spiritual teacher or its teaching we call this 'wise-ing up'. Please do it. Try it. It will not hurt or cost a dime. It's to enlighten a soul of its burdens and ignorance or hardship where either love or peace or both concerns our welfare and that of others.

Why do people hate to love? Nonsense at best. Being put to the test as to whether a person wants to be in a position of right will show if they are unconscious or not. Don't fight with them. All this is 'to be.' Allow the situation for the sake of gracing the moment in peace as oppose to resenting or hatred in return.

"Who wants love like this? Why bother? You'll lose," most will argue. "Foolishness at best!" some retort. Most will take their stance as being the one that's to be accrued to. Well, possibly you are the one in charge ~ so go ahead. Fight away. Hate. Love is the loser, again. Remember the rules, though ~ hate begets war whereby love begets peace in a truism of pristine wisdom.

Hurt, pain or suffering come out of allowing ignorance to do its dirty job. Somebody has to be stupid in life's 'drama' sector. Since we're all already suffering from a lack of concern for the other to win, let's just all fight our way to the top of nowhere in particular except to exasperate the existing pain, then.

Crying is a mode of conduct used by most that would be construed as inferior yet these ones are the mighty giants of love today existing among mankind. They are in the forefront of a battle to be won by soulless people without guilt for their insensitive nature. To be true to their nature is wise among mankind then, true? Start anywhere but with the truth and we stall into ineffective life. Quality counts to the soul as oppose to pretenses proposed due to society's norm to 'get tough' or another one 'crying is for big sissies.' These are untrue euphuisms. 'Might makes right' is too.

Have you cried for someone lately that was in need of assistance of a soul but for lack of concern by humanity was turned away and let down just to be made wrong, weak or given a status as lazy or useless to nobody because they're down and out, maybe again.

Take a bird for example. Say it landed and someone harmed its wing so that flight was permanently affected on this lowly creature. Who cries for it? Does it even matter today in our hardened society as if the creature were of less worth than a soul elsewhere?

If we as a society are sensitive to our need for substance and clothing and see our needs are met, is it so much to ask if a lowly creature that is helpless and truly in need of solace as the divine being in the 'spark' of its soul be of any less value to our concerns? For this work to be accomplished here on this planet to give to another so as to help and assist the lowly and the weak among mankind, would it be too much to ask for assistance to date? Could we show divine grace and favor to another in need of our help?

What of hunger? Is it okay to teach selfishness any longer then we already have as a species? Being sad about the situation helps. It helps when we are moved somehow to inch away from our comforts. Television is fun but so is a walk in the park. Can young children be given more time so that they can see the sun today? Their playful, laughing giddy nature is here to stay so could we lend it our awareness today? Sustain it rather than whisk them away to another dull drum rehearsal with our already overburdened, overtaxed situation opposed by norms we consider 'civilized' at best. Are their hearts filled with blessed joy or overwhelmed by busy overscheduled activity to their detriment? Harm is caused through over exhaustion. Who cares if they are over wrought with pain, agony or fear for their future welfare? Should not their joy, too be taken into consideration from our busy schedule?

What is missed if we don't? Let's consider schools with no recess much less music, art and gym missing now from many schools. In joyless existence they are overwrought with fear alone. Love is a muscle of the heart. Do we fear love or joy so much to be okay with this happening to them too? What of love for mankind? Never mind. I'd be construed as 'pushy' as some would have me be named.

To every event there is a season. This is our season to help someone hopelessly out of sorts with the rest of life. What will that take? Who'll set the goal? Who said everything was not alright? Cry for no one, then. Blind eyes see what concerns its needs alone. No need for pointing fingers if the qualifying loser is us without love. That's how it happens.

Peace yourself with compassion it's dear friend for it's the children of the world who are generally sorted to be among the last to get our media attention. Our compassion as a whole needs an overhaul. The seat of mercy is between our chest. Feel a child's distress, we win in our humanity as wisdom is from above, yes?

Was yesterday busy for you? It was for all those who are in need of getting the job done according to today's standard of right. But as a species mankind, would it help or harm our young of the next generation to see the sun go down without so much as a bright smile in the direction of its sunrise or sunsets so brilliance their form for the sole purpose of giving us a happy existence?

What of grace? It is lovely, too. It's full of wisdom and good. Who is in need of good from another or a kind word or just a happy environment? For such is the way of wisdom.

But to the dismay of most of society in its fast moving, fast pace mode of existence little to none of grace or its beauty is exposed. Through rush and haste, no one is pleased with neither themselves or with the way life's performance is manifesting. Try love silly, what do we have to lose?

"Our sanity is strained," some retort. Still, others square away at being content to watch the madness from afar without so much as lifting a finger to assist an overburdened, overtaxed Mother. Her duties are endless. Beast on our planet are not to whence over our situation, heavy and burdened as it is. It is of those of loving countenance to see and respond as it should happen, for the whole gamut includes those kind and wise as well as those stupefiedly clothed with indifference to getting an obvious need cared for.

Love one another is a must, or don't. Either way we get what we earn. (...deserve some say) We keep moving is what happens. So move we will. The pain will deepen as too our despair or we will use love and lessen it. The equation is motionless, whereas the factor is movement – us as humanity.

A wise choice suffices.

Let's look at that again, Mothers overworking themselves. Do they do it because they want to be overworked to a fault? Is not the 2:00 and 4:00 and 6:00 a.m. feeding caring for the soul of another as they should?

(Hint, hint, hint: Fellows, the ladies are in trouble. Burnout happens from excessive worry quicker on a schedule with children in tow.)

Sorry guys, I need to sell books. So, hummm...I'll just say maybe the ladies overwork themselves to a fault for fun and huh...because babies are their territory like it or not and huh...because they like a burnt-out look as oppose to being normal or supported by its spouse.

Okay, I got myself out of that one, I think. (whew!) There are two sides to every issue folks. I'm still going to have to stay clear from the ladies for that one for at least a year and I'm on their side! The delicate nature of balance, my eye! Yes, ladies you are mightily overworked, overscheduled and overwhelmed. There, I said it.

That's going to cost me a year's worth of revenue. Peace have your way with me, though.

On bent knee where? Within our hearts so within we'll go and reason till sanity means compassion for the lowly and tender with their hearts in tow before a parade of our grown society to manage since babies cry for a need to be satisfied. Crying causes pain not the other way around so though it's in pain its anger is understood, for an angry rebuff from a baby or child suffices. "Somebody better get it!" they all retort.

Our whole existence and even more then our happiness being at stake or our planet is the ability to differentiate that the purpose of your being is just to love that you're alive. Where is this place? Does it exist? Why the pain or its confusion with its suffering of it for even one second?

When a baby cries does it matter? Ask any woman. A woman will answer the call due to its nature to understand even the minute of its need in a whimper.

Why do horses draw carriages? In a time of need they were used to assist in an urgent message that would assist its message bearer. Thus the metaphor to help and assist the lowly among mankind. Eventually that person is you one way or another. Give to another what can be helped through a stance of sufficiency. Can you feel love in her fullness? Many, most cannot. Where the giver's of mankind?

Why are we selfish in our need to give? Suppose everyone were indifferent to the needs of others? (gulp.) Where would we get the necessary care for our soul?

Let's imagine that the earth were flat. What kind of planet would mankind accrue to for its substance? Impossible true, yet that is the way mankind is living today. People everywhere are not getting the proper nourishment and appropriate satisfaction living in a broken environment. Life therefore is not linear but rather it contends itself on moisture from the planet as well as any or all living species do.

Let's accrue to the rainforest. Everyone loves to be able to have for their substance enough for their soul. Yet in the rainforest their moisture in the way of running rivers are damp or completely dried to the bone. Is this what humanity calls 'giving' attention to the needs of the planet as with when water holes exposed it makes the plant life die and makes for heavy cartilage to the existing wildlife? These souls abiding in the forest love their environment, true? They live in a round environment as oppose to the linear environment of the fast pace city loud, noisy environment of modern living.

This is not a book about the abandonment of what 'is'. Cities hold their glory lot as man has built them for their glory alone to the exclusion of the way nature is accepting of her mode.

Can cities be beautified in the meantime while the rest of humanity comes to its senses? The world holds billions of opportunities in this area as far as suggestions that may be proposed. On occasion can an area be left for the earth to recover rather then automatically build a train station or a sky scraper or a building with little or no meaning where the earth and her recovery is at stake?

Certainly cities have their functions. Many are beautiful still to date to the eye of illusion, though. Why not help society by being alert to the needs of all of creation and her simplicity rather then to a complicated, complex environment as a city imposes upon us as creatures of our habitat.

Noise is harmful to the environment. So too is the overcrowding of her resources on her. Planet earth is a pristine jewel of beauty. What is it to our species if she is crushed and bruised? To whom does it matter today? Why should we bother? Would it not cost us in the areas of either currency exchange planetarily or in a way we feel and think to date?

When the earth is in crisis as she is today let's all as a species be as sensitive as possible in any way that matters to accept the situation that we are presented with. Humanity has a kind streak. Yes, even a lowly cardinal is susceptible to the winds of change whether they move swiftly or too low a current for it to soar for appropriate landing and taking off. Sometimes even these simple procedures for the winged ones in our heavenly spaces are affected tremendously too and permanent even, dissatisfaction to their disliking much as any human is affected by the cruelty or misguidance of bad managers of our earthly home.

Everyone has a voice. Use your senses to see if your environment is satisfied with the next planned move you feel you will take for the sake of the children who will be left with the job too to care for their homeland in a state of grace.

I saw a red rose
and gave it a name
of red, green, yellow
and blue.
Save it for later
to talk of its color,
is greater than
me and you.

Cry

Do you want to be starting somethin'?

Why do doves cry? To get the attention of anyone sensitive to its needs. If I cry do you feel my pain? Of course not and I cry often. This is not my usual attire to be sensitive. I grew up a rough and tough girl with all the misgivings being young had to offer. My stature was that of an athletic person. I coursed my soul to be in every win / lose competition to ever challenge my every endeavor to come out a winner, to see the victory for myself which happened often and losing rarely never.

In reading literature too, I looked for wisdom to wise myself up so I would have an internal guide. I didn't hold true to it, for youth always challenged my inner soul to rebuff what seemed normal from outward appearance. I read the bible more times than anyone on this planet I suppose, with its light to awaken my darkened soul when I faltered. I read many authors on their experiences with 'light' and its love and understood the journey to awareness is through our conscious being held true to itself. I have yet to find a book to hold to the Power of Now, though.

Good news spreads like wildfire, I suppose. Good for me then to wise myself up to yet another profound deeply wise soul. I took everything I had grown to understand about Christ, Eckhart Tolle, apostles of old… you name it and rolled every last one of them up and held them up to the 'light of consciousness' I had borne witness to. Eckhart Tolle was my last stop. I got off the train of being a spiritual seeker permanently. That's how absolute and clear his teaching was presented.

I figuratively went to the river shortly thereafter and rolling up 'within' all the wisdom I had accrued to that point I tossed it out to the universe. I knew I would receive an answer from life Itself on what would be true from this last gesture of peace to become conscious.

I wanted to become and be in the infinite girdle of truth in One mode. To be conscious was an admirable enough goal to seek especially since love seemed likeable enough with its momentary awareness. It was the answer for me at all cost. The result nullifies my fear so true to my need to be worthy of its sum that in infinity 'within' the answer came, an added bonus this book as a result of seeing a need to help people to affect a permanent change of heart on a whim. Consciousness effects change so I wanted in for that to happen, too.

The ability to awaken up to truth again transposed before my life. Good riddance to the old mode. Now I'm more likened to an infinite consciousness aware of 'light' and love and can beam awareness at will. To transpose the physical existence, love is required. Not an optional outlet for some, for many still are conditioned with the old order and its loud, contentious mode, still.

Stillness is silence of the mind. Thought is still, not ruffled nor hurried. The turtle/ rabbit scenario suffices its theme be of its word or a situation or a person.

As a young girl I had fallen in love literally with Christ when around 11' ish years old. I wanted him to marry me when I grew up so I would not have to suffer my heart becoming broken when it was time for me to find a true love. I knew if I married his soul he would be loyal, trustworthy and a kind person who would never break my heart with the usual problem of fooling around with any other woman and keeping his love true for only me alone through life. I told this to no one.

Relationship for relationship, I wanted to keep mine on a track since all I saw were girls getting their hearts broken only. I figured in my 11 year old heart, "Hey, these girls aren't doing it right, not like I'm going to. Love is a piece of cake!" (...or so I thought.)

Time passed. Again, I held fast to my heart never to expose what I truly felt about males who would break a heart for nothing more then being selfish. But what hurt worst is watching some of the most beautiful women this planet has ever held have their hearts broken for our existence seemed worth nothing, even 'less than nothing' at times when needing a male to respond with a higher character ~ like wisdom. I sense males and their agitation with the female, mostly.

Men would chose to cheat on their significant other without so much of getting the whole picture of what transpires in our heart when infidelity happens to us makes me wonder again and again as I've seen the same disillusionment played over four decades now. I've come to learn men feel woman are the snare but I beg to differ.

So I went back to my, "I want to marry Christ" mode as when I was 11 years old, "No broken heart this way," I told myself in earnest! When I was eleven, I had a dream with the intent to have a pure, wholesome relationship with all the joy life had to offer. This too I learned the hard way is idealism in today's world of broken hearts, families and homes. Still my heart knew what it wanted, take no prisoners. Then, along came Eckhart Tolle just as sweet in his soul of christ-like stature yet here on earth with wisdom enough for the whole planet! I looked up to heaven and retorted, "You've got to be joking, right!?"

So, it was true. Life could produce beauty incarnate in a male. I had bought Eckhart Tolle's now world famous book The Power of Now and after reading every passage like the gospel it was, I returned to the cover page and stared at his picture and it accompanied an inner voice that warned yet consoled, "He's taken sweetie, but I got you right here with Me, still."

I knew it was the higher Intelligence of wisdom telling me to drop the infatuation. Yet, life did produce a beautiful male at last, couldn't refute the evidence! The crush continued for a few years so I'm over that bump.

So I said, "The lord's up there and Eckhart Tolle's down here but indisposed. What's next?" due to a heart has a mind of its own plus mine wanted a pure conscious counterpart male to assist and support my journey as an equal yet undeniably beautiful soul for the storms of life to be buffered alongside myself to share a common love for the divine together.

I'm still growing in awareness. Translation: A male has a way of being, unconscious or otherwise so pick a wise mate when you chose. Like my present spouse, he dislikes everything divine in its source. Yet like wisdom has taught us, yoke with a dummy you get what you deserve.

My kids were in love with their Daddy so I stayed a bit in the marriage to see whole their hearts and keep them from having to experience coming from a broken family. I loved them enough to suffer in silence. I'm glad I stayed keeping the family intact otherwise I would have experience them with a broken heart ~ my worst nightmare.

My children have now grown with one the last child leaving and packing as I speak. I feel the winds of change calling me in a new adventure which may or may not include their Dad who I'll sorely miss. Friends to the end though, he and I. Now I belong in that group of us billion or so girls out there looking for mature 'true' love. I'm in that fun group, (gulp).

Looking back my three children hated the wisdom I had come to know as '*inner awareness*' to my shock and dismay. I want them safe out there in that big old world all alone. I don't want their hearts broken as mine has, nor to search for something that will only hurt their heart being a broken family home or love withheld by a selfish mate as power struggles are predominately male in nature due to mind with its empty chatter along with what Eckhart wrote of so eloquently of the mind with its destructive, mad and insane way of behaving and considered 'normal' by our society and the world over.

The book came out just in time, as I taught my three girls to never give in to these qualities of self-destruct but rather go with love alone for the sake of their sanity. They are in need to wise up their heart to escape the beast of selfishness accrued as the norm or be hurt by it ~ as life lessons are pearls of wisdom. Its life saying, "You goofed yet still got the rest of your life to go. Do not try to change a stripe, go with a smooth clear surface with its circle in excellence and wisdom. Love be your guide, as infinite is a soul. Match love on its terms and know better."

Though I put on a tough exterior, when alone most of the time I cry because humanity is too far off course to hear beauty or have time for it like in a beautiful one of a kind sky which each day has tried to get the attention in every way it could to no avail.

I see it now and I love that the sky is of One. It sings and plays and notices everything, too. Like the proverbial rose that is adorned no less than the skies or a tree, we have become so attuned to the tragic rather then listen to the beauty they expound that even tears from heaven are considered fake.

Heaven cries? Yes. When, for what purpose? Who would care anyway? What if there was no Higher Intelligence that felt or cared about humans like we say happened? What if that were true? Angels appear surely enough amidst our presence. Plenty of books abound on their character. There are other books with lies that abound, proliferate even.

But what if that were true once ~ that heaven above didn't care? One time only? What would happen to this order of magnificent as it is although people care less that it's cared about unknown to their ears and eyes literally. The result would be a disaster to life. Not from the standpoint of mankind but from the standpoint of the purpose of why we came into existence and for whom.

Some call it god, others depersonalize its friendship with "Hey, got to run. Some other time. So long!" But what if it mattered little to us to the point of our humanity was stopped as it is on this level? What then?

The power of wisdom affords Itself to give us, a weary species a turn to face rather than deny or resist an open invitation to desist our folly and be patient with our correction of being dumber than a fish swimming upstream in the fall. Backwards as being nasty in temperament is and as good as it is to be right at some point or another ~ let's suppose for the sake of being kind we decide to be One with peace and understand our role as peacemaker. What form would we be holding up to the light of consciousness so we can see the result before we take that next step, the only one that exist (…by the way) according to those who are privileged to understand the nature of the spirit?

Would it look like people killing each other just to prove a point or would it look like what we know would transpire ~ a world with love calling the shots. Bury your head in the ground, shut your eyes and hope it all goes away soon is not going to happen.

To hear a baby cry is not a crime, not to the one who birthed the precious being. To any other, the child has a distant relationship at best with it. What of a mother who wants, needs and gets so little response to the most precious expression of life here on our planet? Where our compassion which is just as good as any place to begin in our growth of the soul with its 'inward journey' toward enlightenment? A baby peaces humanity with its presence, a rose by any other name or what of an ant stepped on out of careless miss observation as being not strong yet so have your way or dismissal of its soul as insignificant among us. That is not the way of the One. I mode a bee, myself. For they get us first. It's their nature. Why? To prove we are second not first where what matters counts in our big scheme of "What's in it for me?" again. Do it. Lucky you, man. Not everybody likes a fool. Wisdom yourself with peace for babies and fools are cute but who wants to be the latter? Everybody's got a gun in America. Notice our dwindling entry for residency anybody?

Why cry if someone else hurts? I unfortunately do it all the time not due to anything physically being amiss among people of the earth per say, but I cry because of the nonsense and its deliberate forgoing of peace for the sake of 'somebody wants to be right' rather than forego their side of an all important issue such as me/my/our win verses your goal.

It works for some but in the long run, hatred superfluously rears itself to our heart as making sense when actually it's the opposite that happens. Life is simple enough when love remains our focus. Yet, to date love has all but vanished. Where the kind words? The kind acts of compassion? A moved spirit to speak wise instead of conformity due to fear?

Mankind is alone in their one-sided lopsided issue where peace matters.

Watch water...literally. It conforms, bends and offers itself willingly in peaceful attire for the benefit of all living beings. So beat up, beaten down and surrender yet worthy her wisdom as we still take from her which harms her being rather than compassionately assist her on a road to recovery. If we want to heal the planet and our species, please be open to any opportunity to assist even this lowly compassionate situation.

Being compassionate is situational exactly as '*Is*' for humanity is selfish and selfless in One. But if being selfish for the sake of convenience rather than for a loving purpose as according to Oneness then we suffer in anguish, its usual outcome.

"What would love do now?" means little. I've seen that one in action too with little avail. Wisdom, it's the answer. Talk suffices a deadbeat. Action that covers a need cures whereby talk dismisses it.

The dissatisfaction of talking about being lonely or aloneness as some have jargoned the terms are just words. For those pained by its existence and it is true there are many and so few in between that are smarting due to a lack of experience with the opposite sex that even males themselves are enthralled by his counterpart the female and stumped by her beauty. Beauty suffices and going 'within' helps. But to affect a cure for loneliness either with or without a partner, go 'within' in either circumstance. The outcome is peace.

On with life we go as '*Is*' as usual. Movement is a part of what has to be, too. And a big one! Stillness counters movement. One withstands the other. Like a tree overrun with ant mounds near her trunk, touchy situation a male with a female together. Modern life is hectic, stressful and in wisdom give space to one another. (...a.k.a also known as clinginess. Give one another room. Being suffocated by a person romantic or not isn't healthy on the psyche.)

Some feel there will never be that special someone to hold, talk to and cherish. Even these lonely hearts want to know what does evolving consciousness have to do with the immediate demands of finding a mate while the planet is in need of our assistance with its dire cry for help. Well, slow down a bit. Everything is happening for a reason, I can assure you. Love is a really big topic, not only in demand for the young among humanity but also a legitimate concern for parents and grandparents alike who soon will be off the world scene yet are concerned for those loved who will be left to carry societies burdens with its needs.

There is a balance here, too. In the young, patience is of upmost importance. Yet and still being of tender countenance and true impatient to find that 'one and only' there tends to be a tug at the heart for all concerned. In youth, patience is hearsay of those up in years with their trial and errors on the matter mostly behind them. What is ahead for these overtaxed youth worldwide where it concerns them most ~ on their approaching adulthood yet still without a suitable mate to comfort the sore spots life tends to toss their fragile souls in this area alone?

Youth has its privileges. In young adults it's their resilience to face challenges with gusto as oppose to sitting back waiting for that certain someone to tug their heart sufficient enough to vow marriage to. What of family life and children and rearing them in these days where so few are able to get appropriate sufficient funds let alone a good night's rest to charter a wise course within reason?

Love bites. So let's reason along the lines where it affects growth in the soul, first. Love is not for the faint of heart. Love requires stamina unknown before the situation presents itself. If you have thick skin, hooray. Same goes for the touchy-feely sort. Endure your relationship if you're in one as oppose to jumping quickly to a solution that can lead to excruciating pain in the future.

Where is that one for me, though? Many adults would rather be young again to retry the situation. Too late, though. Go from where you are. Proceed with caution with your senses up rather than a hormonal choice which currently amounts to abuse on the soul needlessly.

Whenever we go against the tide of reality something aspires that will seem amiss. "Can't put your finger on it, though," as that's the retort of those experienced to its folly's of leap before one looks at the situation deeply enough.

Contrary to popular demand, love is as it should be right at this moment. Wisdom dictates we be patient with our young in society. Will their cry also go unheard by the masses once again in their busy-ness of getting along with the necessities of life? What a conundrum! For life in its wisdom always manages to surface right when we all need something bigger and bolder to challenge our missteps where wisdom was excused yet once again for the sake of 'our' convenience and I use the term lightly.

Over and above the call of duty our young have bared our stripes of indifference. Love has a powerful ability to intoxicate the listener ~ be it in form or its formless condition.

Suppose one day we all woke up and love was never to be found. In our unevolved, unenlightened state, humanity has become as though sightless to ones most in need of its assistance.

Today is wisdom's mercy seat of observance being expounded, yet by some tolerated once again in the name of "Who the heck you referring to lady, me?" one more time. In the 'what comes around goes around' mode, we as society will never get out of the stagnate current of lovelessness, then. Stay with it, love has its privileges.

To those that love being at peace, there is hope still. Love wants and needs to be heard. "A voice in the wilderness," some retort. Hummm... maybe. Still, wisdom is the answer. Going 'within' is the duty of One, true? If a day seems rotten to you then say something in reverse order like the "Turn Around" method being expounded by brilliant spiritual teacher Byron Katie who had a sudden spiritual awakening as myself and Eckhart Tolle.

The 'first the pain then the answer mode' is playing out in our society. There are many good teachers these days to help us as I've mentioned. There's of course again Eckhart Tolle a modern day miracle at the helm of his teaching. The wisdom he propounds upon society is beyond the beauty we experience as peace with its by-product as wisdom. Here too conventional wisdom gets its way above wisdom in its absolute. Peace eludes many to a fault, still. Ready yet, humanity?

Pain and suffering are words. In 'One' mode we all have a say, not just a majority group here or there. Wisdom is divine. What of its source which is not in business mode rather just being loving or lovely as a day on the beach? The wind blows for a reason as does an ocean tide carry its currents in a circle and not in linear mode. (...laymen translation: to listen with your heart ~ not the mind.)

These teachings are unique and unknowable to the thinking soul. It's go with the heart and its good or bust. Their teachings are simple enough but as for the direction it produces on our awareness, more is less in One.

What good is a spiritual teacher if the situation is left to wander then fall by the wayside? Do you pray? Prayer along with action is the key. A prayer is words, true yet unless accompanied to assist people to recognize their hand in the matter counts, we'll get nowhere. What of our heart? Feeling sorry counts, I guess. A flick of a remote can get an entire generation to discount a plea from a child on the tube. How distant we have become to our species!

Look again, an angel is wingless, too. Some purport from the above area of consciousness to this realm to assist, true as we are part of the whole ~ One with everything, too. Look at your hand, what do you see? Assistance at the next turn or a run to the fridge for ice cream?

Nothing wrong with treats for a soul but what of legitimate hunger facing humanity? The solution comes with effort to eliminate and solve the matter least we pull a cover over our eyes of compassion and doze way off course to the issue humanity has at its doorstep. All it takes is a look. Look away again, then. It's easy, comfortable even. What if it were you next time that needed that favor? What right does life have to 'giddy up' to the pace of what matters to a few with the exclusion of another. It won't. We understand it works that way. What superhuman being is going to land from up there to transport us from our stupor if not words of wisdom or compassion? Same old story.

Okay. Let's go into resistance once more and let the beautiful among mankind those who serve a higher purpose say lawyers, doctors and political affiliates excuse themselves from Oneness till some other issue comes along that will 'fit' a realistic schedule ~ one that includes harmony for some and others for injustice to rule its area with blind consequences.

For if the divine whole includes this higher intelligence of all encompassing compassion, then let's all wait for that answer. It does help. But let's try that one on:

"Hello, my name is Mr._____. I'd love to but I have a business to run. Please society, excuse me from my weary schedule. More of this again tomorrow, I can assure you!" And so on down a road of indifference we go.

And so those who could be helped are passed over. Change affects the many whereas status quo will ruin a date to an effective cure. Being tired and lost is a good excuse, humanity. But in the name of 'waking up spiritually' it suffices nothing but the pocketbook and our convenience.

How does this change from Oneness to a fractured society stuck on being a deadbeat and beat-up situation for once? Besides, love that is?

Look inwardly, for the answer is 'within.' Love has no form. It's felt as being able to accomplish with little or no effort ~ just a willing ear to participate in the most magnificent part of our existence once more for the sake of such loving members of society, like a flower unnoticed.

Was it hard? Do you need lessons to do it right? Does someone look at a flower better then you and so an argument ensues over the correct way to look at its blessed beauty? Argue over something be it a plant an issue or a person, the heart is equal its sum. It is the fruit of One. Don't argue then is the answer. Peace all with love (…as within so without) with beauty your core right, so as to effect a purpose worthy our humanity.

Please, be kind inwardly. See, no effort and no harmful after effects to throw our planet into some uncopeable whirlwind again. Simple, see? Love and truth is all we have to admire in anyone or circumstance which presents itself…for wholeness is just that, us being nice again. (… whew!)

Nice has its privileges beyond being truth worthy. Held to the light of consciousness love is all we got. Give generously! You don't have to like another person to try it out. It works best when resisted on every level you possibly can try it out on, say like yourself.

What better person to get involved with a change of heart with if not your inner soul aligned with good ~ for its benefits are truly immeasurable much like love and compassion their counter parts.

Trust whom, where or when? Nowhere in particular. In 'One' mode the trusted party is just as good as the one issuing the situation to be trusted. Just be there as its recipient for no other reason than to get nowhere in particular other than to win / lose by default. There is no reason to accrue to, love just bends and flows and who knows where?

It's better to give into the unknowingness of any situation rather than give into some higher personage of infinite being into lord only knows what reality will reveal and assure ably it will because the One works on this premise. Heading into an infinite being to see what? To do it how? Where? It can't happen! The premise is faulty to the seat of reason. The outcome is observed for the sole purpose to see what the original purpose is that put the entire chain of events into motion then observe / give Its observation that that is the answer.

"Well okay then," says the doubting mind at last. I speak in *Absolute*. There is no one with this ability. It's just a special gift to humanity so they will be healed of what matters for their future to aspire to goodness. So be of love this time, okay?

Again, choice rules, ours at that. Wake up! Smell you in a rose. For by any other name you are better than life being put on paper or in a rose. To stop life from happening is impossible. The higher personage that is of Its own intelligence sees wisdom incarnate as oppose to being a ruler or dictator or nay-sayer.

What if It did say "No," ever? What would transpire is against conventional wisdom so the result would suffice as no sun, no moon, no form everywhere ~ all because *It* is also form and formless, see?

Easy. Remember to be wise and say, 'Yes'. Wisdom suffices a generation as lost as we have become. Most spiritual teachers will talk until blue in the face for fear its audience will self-destruct on its own behalf to what end? Perhaps a nice day will work for once. "We hope," say those truly awaken at least to notice we are situational in existence as oppose to putting ourselves out of existence with a trusted, "Please, don't do that." We watch in earnest then, as life is situational at best.

Don't clog leaves in a drain. We're the clogged pipe. Please assist in the removal of a leaf, if just one. Pipes are meant to be drained not clogged like ants are meant for busyness offering the wisdom humans are meant to cooperate not suffocate nature with our nonconformity. Cooperating with the planet means going along with her and not squandering her to the degree of extinction.

Again ~ trust is the issue. Mankind has a role to play. For our part, in order for wisdom to manifest itself in pristine clearness as oppose to a murky doubt of pessimism, be of 'One' where the air is so clean, so clear and so pure that to discount it would be stupefied incarnate. Now, truth both exist side by side with folly. Wasn't a time when that one never existed. Remember oil/water meow/bark clean/messy. This is 'One' or suffices to say one's meaning. It's wisdom in our choice, wisdom in creation or any circumstance and yet for the sake of repeating the obvious both love and its inseparable counter partner wisdom are 'within' being us and we for It is you or I. Again, if they're nice ~ pick these as the choice of the future.

To discount an obvious reality such as sweet/sour heavy/light and nice/mean spirited is to stay in the slow lane of wisdom's understanding.

Children run to happy folk and hide away from those they sense can harm or bring them to tears. Self preservation rules in the young as oppose to some of us older folk with our 'I got to pay this off at any cost' mentality. Unfortunately the result can be disastrous to a soul willing to conform to a budget well out of its scope to recoup what's already loss to trillions of dollars say like our everyday economy has been for decades worldwide.

Silly us to try and we will for we must. Okay, I'll stop talking if we as

One stop providing so, so, so much material to do ten or a hundred more such books on, "I know we stupefied a moment of peace but hey, everybody went along, too!" No culprits then, yes? Finger-pointing amounts to as a no-show to love again if we do that.

Someone may hurt my feelings because my being sensitive could 'break a bone' rather than scream and punch the heck out of society for the sake of getting us moving toward love for the sake of being good.

Pause.

Still within. (meaning: *me as peace*.)

Silence.

(…deep breathing. Overwhelming situation is only a moment. Smile at the kitty walking past me in awareness. Come here kitty. Help me help the audience with awareness in not making a sound unless need be. Like purring but that's only because you're sweet. Like we ought to but won't because as being human somehow we just can't make a transaction into a bliss so beautiful that even a rainbow would cry in pain to see our sorryful existence so away from what love represents. Never mind…)

Let's stay pitiful unconscious, limit ourselves in what we're aware of that makes sense to everybody like love being kind and get back to No-thing. We are It. Awareness. Did a fish out there in existence want to know the depth of the water it's swimming in again once more just in case it runs short of water on the planet? Could it happen? Perhaps.

We demolished the largest body of water in the form of a sea basin in Africa. Who knows? Anything is possible, you think? Does being realistic help or hurt the situation?

Who gets to choose our situation of what matters? Looks like we're doing a good job in answering that. Look around. Does hell resemble life or is it the other way around? Could both be true at this point of our situation? Would you like to (hold on here…I'll rephrase the moment as peace it 'is'.)

I'll rephrase this situation which is a silly statement. Would we like to try peace and love if we called it '***Change***'? (whew!...now I got to hope I don't get assassinated.) Love or peace humanity, please.

There is a divine, sacred grace looming in the area of it. (**...**I reiterate, I hope nobody comes after me to shoot me. I like my existence. I know you do, too. So if just one person out there benefits, my short-lived existence will be well worth a scandal of the century. Wonder the likes of us wanting to know "Who shot the peace monger?" Like the thriller, "Who shot J.R?" you know?)

Our situation in peace is almost as hilarious.

I am for change, though. I love the idea of world peace. Cooperation is the key to our harmonious existence which we don't have. There are holy passages that talk about it, remember? What say us, we try?

So the choice is ours at every moment but we all forgot that's what presence represents. Why? How? Who knows?

I wasn't meditating a moment ago. I fainted briefly. Just a passing thought someone out there actually listened and felt a change of heart to be (gulp) nice. "Perish the thought!" while scrambling, murmured the status quo sector. See? What did I say? For the sake of reiterating the rules, "Good affects change." To better whom, though? Us as the One.

So good, then. To choose otherwise, go back to the end of the line, do not pass go and be cheap on affection. Good for you, we all lose for we are all...(gulp) you. One has the way of transpiring what is true. Wisdom wakes up those ready for change.

Where love abides, there are fewer if ever headaches, migraines or overwrought burdened back strains. The 'our budget's' being at the helm is a crying shame as we're exhausting our will to continue on our way in peaceful co-existence with everything to be One with all. Love everything, hate everything. It's alright ~ it's the same in One. Life is fair. Choice counts, keep up. Don't look back least we add another thought of illusion to our pocketbooks, emotions and not to mention our well being with our already squeezed out, burnt-out overbearing schedules we deal with to date attest to we all are in need of much rest.

Love me, please. What does that mean as I / me / you are One and have never been separated from the cause of our existence ever?

Love. Sit with it, be agreeable in countenance as oppose to ever wanting to be one up or right. Say 'yes' to love as though it is the only recourse for humanity. Love be of One, then.

In another book I will refer to the "What if…" game as the psyche will transpose much on the issue of 'What if we do love as One?' and 'What will happen to our selfish hateful attire?' I guess that pretty much answers it in a nutshell. And one more my personal favorite, "What if I love myself and another as the same me/myself/ in One?"

In truth the answer is and always was what will be. What will transpire will look a lot like a remission of lust otherwise known as greed in any kind be it of the formless condition or of its form in a physical sense. Love be us then, in a return to our humanity.

Who wants to trust me / yet you / rather us just this once?

Who are we in our construct to deny our sole this one mercy, to be wisdom incarnate in One? Silly universe to accept if we refuse but would it suffice us as a species to do so? Harmony at best is a word yet when used 'within' it becomes incarnate 'us' too. That makes two nice assets, see? Try it, love won't bite. Nibble, maybe. Then perhaps we'll be soothed by its bathing lighter air of our existence at some near as oppose to a distant future for us.

Today wisdom comes to us in the form of not saying 'No' to anything but rather 'Yes' with the power of might leading our humanity. Might in her truer sense, that is.

In wisdom itself I was born to delight as 'Yes' accrues to the above realm due to its characteristic of dignity with its stealth to move in One as about and within the earth, within wind as 'yes' charters her course through mankind and 'yes' of course motioning planetary and otherworldly spacial orbits orchestrating midst our vast depthless universe from within, too. 'Yes' holds true to itself time and again as being realistic is nowhere to be found except within wisdom.

As special as love is and we being that special vessel in One mode, humanity will suffice itself on the sweet only or with just little or no bitterness. "Look away, run and whatever you do, don't be a positive person!" This the banner of our unconscious existence. Say goodbye to it.

The books to be release come so as to accept its wisdom as well as its truth is what will be introduced as what use to be called in Genesis, the *Tree of Eternal Life*. What's being expounded is wisdom personified otherwise known as The One for who else can be clear as crystal in its wisdom of understandment for we as society are in need of love to accrue to our best circumstance to arise. Love is painless as oppose to the loveless situation we have imposed upon our spirit to date. With that I'll proceed with caution for who but we are being wised up to become good once more. And good is a relative term to sum up our dilemma as a whole lot of noise compared to our common garment of peace known as silence due to its greater place in our being.

Wisdom for all is just a fairytale to those unwilling to proceed for what's best for everyone. Being selfish had its season. Maturity dictates a reasonable reply without coercion or chastisement. (…in laymen's terms, if you have to twist their arm using force, its effectiveness at best was truly not worthy of your insistence for change.) Change is the order of *highly evolved beings.*

HEB's are the norm among the sane. With growth comes noticeable improvement as well as its counter holding true for going against wisdom is beyond bottoming out on society. Take charge, though. Be One with the kind, happy you first. Be a model of wisdom and enliven an area once trodden down with over burden us drama.

It's human to go into denial and refuse to feel we as a whole are divine in nature. "I haven't seen love or truth or got a fair break at anything in my life!" some may in chagrin recant to oneself. Well read on, everything changes ~ that's our birthright to know life holds true to the axiom of what goes up must come down. So what comes around (loveless us) goes around (kinder humanity). Its math is loyal see, if nothing else. And the old 'treat others the way you would like to be treated' is not a lesson to become our lot but 'be' our lot instead. A refresher course in love will suffice the situation. The curtain call is for us to stand take the bow and be real that we always had the best performance going on in town, silly humanity of two-ness in defiance of itself yet One disguised as peace. If humanity wasn't mostly peaceful then the truism of us being off center is just as true but take a closer look at every second, year and our total history from the start of creation and our peace time over-shadowed its temporary warlike countenance (for realistic reasons, we're only human with all its mishaps) graced with divine presence our greater lot.

'Do not argue with reality' as Byron Katie has touch on its truism, 'for you will only lose 100 % of the time.'

We have been free to choose to be sweet and we chose it already. Keep up the good is an oxymoron statement, see? More waking up to this moment will be presented in book form only. Our spiritual awakening is upon us, mankind. (...whew! Being nice has its merits.)

We never needed me to produce three books to transpire for the betterment of one soul let alone an entire generation in struggle with itself. "In love I produced a baby," said the couple. Who produced me to speak is humanity. You're doing this to yourself ~ demanded, even for this moment to transpire.

For the ones smart enough to leave off the formal approach to wisdom and having to read it by instead knowing wisdom is already your lot, we all applaud your insight to not need any other publication on love to be a necessity. For the rest of you among mankind feeling shafted due to sensing you didn't receive your fair share of love from others due to a shortage of nasty mean-spirited souls among us then please, follow me to book 3.

Instruction awaits. Love procures a healing through its commonsense approach by taking wisdom by the hand this time, mankind. Whatever you do, stay close to normal people as normal is relative to strange bottomed-out (for lack of a better word...) low life's. Peaceful folk like us are their safety nets, thus it's hard to get rid of them once they bond with us. Seems too when they are among like-kindred spirits of the tricky folk they are, they make so little headway there. So out to the nicey gullible innocent along with us being its frenzy feeding ground. I reiterate I must say it like this so as to prevent your kindness which is construed as weakness in the weak-minded from being taken advantage by others without regret.) I'm sure people want to be good at heart, follow me to naive land just the same. So, let's say for the sake of expediency our commonsense in its truth open wider our defense mode in the name of returning to sanity once and for all.

First topic of book three then, "Life is fair" and so follow the rules that hold to deeper wisdom. Everything attracts in One mode for every instance of existence is beauty incarnate, breath being its substance and love its counterpart. The words lack its reality for it is you/us/me back together being One as/with another.

Following then will be chapter 2 in bold face type yet alive as being us presented as, "I took the low road now I'm presented with the high road." For people who are afraid of heights, hold true to a trusted friend.

When most of us get to the top the issue ~ peace, from that vantage point beyond human perception you will be aware of the extra-curricular half of society among us is still way at the bottom of the issue of peace with its drama, peaceless attire causing and occasional 'ouch' moment ~ for your sensitivity will heighten and broaden its scope as peace with awareness becomes an area encompassing your entire being with love being you. Who knew?

We can't see the wind or its strength unless its power is manifested. In name only love 'is' true. (…for the Tolle fans, don't choke) And since in reality the wind is no-thing unbeknownst to you and I the wind is, was and forever will be just that ~ a live being. Being alive then, it laughs out in exasperation to get us to notice it carrying its gentle breezes on beautiful summer evenings and twilighty nights to beseech us to take part and parcel too our kin being sunbeams in their breathless attire and the heavenly starry nights as both put on their one of a kind displays of affection should we chose to pay them our attention.

So congratulations to our young people in society coming of age! We welcome you especially and with open acceptance Oneness is your lot with humanity there to focus attention in love to see you peaced as greater wisdom comes never too late, see?

One

Good morning sunshine
love's in light,
of today's wonderment
work nor right.

Breathless kiss
of wonderment's anew
twice shy, once bitten
thought you knew.

For love just 'is'
when it's on key,
so loosen that tie
follow me

to us sung on key.
For mercy's it
when love is right.
Come! Let's sit.

Love is here to discuss us whole,
better now then never.
One of us is all we have
come highlander nor wither

to move a mighty fortress of hate.
Love alone can do this, never stall.
Hatred falls as scales
from eyes who hear love's call.

Love me too, please

Gulp!

I would like to talk a little about my spiritual awakening. I was having a hard time in my life and anything resembling joy or close to it was sorely missing. I did have a family life yet applying love to anything, anywhere and always where ever I went was tiring it. I was trying to make the 'rules of the heart' work.

I ended up in the spirit realm before the Creator. I thought I was going to stay there in the spirit realm which was okay with me. I liked it for if I thought of something I was given the correct meaning immediately. I felt like such a loser for on planet earth our home I felt I knew so many spiritual truths that I needed no other person but what I had learned from the holy scripture. Yet there at every turn and without letup I was constantly given the truth. I wanted to win with these powerful spirits in assembly looking at me like some important procession was taking place.

I was the center of everyone's wonderment. I could see the earth below which comforted me deeply. Yet I wondered why this interest in me all of a sudden.

I must have won something I thought. Then I dismissed it. I felt favored, blessed though for what? And there was a lot of giggling! Their laughter was constant. I made a face at one of the beings and they stopped, held my hand and it felt like a wave of love to make my existence more likeable. They don't disagree with love.

I felt like a child and everyone was so playful. I attempted to want to take notes of what seemed like an existence much like ours yet so totally different. But I was given notice that such pens or pencil writings were for our earth to explore perhaps examine so we could reach conclusions. 'Conclusions' have no sense there. So that evaporated, too. It was funny I could see multi-dimensional. Where was the warm/cold up/down? It didn't exist for that would be the end of what we call madness. You have to have a 'thing' for such to exist. Loud does not exist there.

I thought of my children I had left behind on earth but again instantly I knew they were on the planet as they should for our existence is taken and examined (which sounds dumb)...through our divine heavenly owner.

Every little thing we do is noted that's why now I like I was returned to the planet. I thought my stay in the spirit realm was it for me yet I was carried back to earth by an angel, a light being of intense study, too for we are all looked upon with keen interest. Some follow the above, most abandon it down here. Yet, love really does matter.

So anyway, the Maker saw I was put in school for seven days and seven nights which I'm figuratively having to speak here because there is light there alone. I studied in a school with many spirit beings.

First I went through a elementary school course and finished that. Secondly I went through a middle school and finished that. I entered what meant a high school spiritual class. Then I was put in a college through a university education where I graduated with a grade point you really do not want me to discuss. It's perhaps much like our PH D education when pursuing excellence so our talent could shine.

I feel as though I have a doctorate for truly our existence on this planet is viewed from above as a place where the soul's growth is its soul purpose.

As I walked about I knew innately there was no end to life per say.

From my school training I became aware of mishaps we were accruing from moving beyond the divine. We need to slow it down a bit.

I'd like to make a few suggestions if I may concerning our present life on the planet. It comes from me, not exactly from above for we are free agents. I notice so many are dying from simple 'stress' related incidents alone. Could we be kinder in this area? Perhaps realizing that stress is a killer especially in our generation as we could go a long ways to alleviate suffering from our planet for too peace means we understand our true purpose of being.

I'd like to suggest yoga too if I may especially due to our fast past, stress filled schedules for it will go a long ways to keep us quiet, heal the soul some and calm our spirit. I would like to mention likewise our eating habits. I notice we take our bodies for granted. Perhaps should we reduce our consumption of meat the planet wide to perhaps 10% and increase our intake of whole grains and fruits along with vegetables being our main consumption, for we could alleviate so many physical ills. Our bodies are attuned to peace. Who of us could have a peaceful sleep loaded with empty calories, non nutrition and these highly packed sugared meals? That could only tire us as a society and even our planet. Balance is truly needed.

I would like to mention also our alternative medicines or perhaps if some could return to the homeopathic way to heal ourselves again instead of consuming chemical drugs which take us off balance where our mind, body and spiritual wholeness concerns us.

I mentioned a few simple solutions we can regain balance. Yes, in truth love is the answer here for to deviate from what truly matters, our soul – it could mean distress.

There are simple pleasures that we have forgotten such as to simply sit quietly or to hold another's hand when ill. When we are love based alone, truly the answers that we need are present without anyone needing, or being in want for any reason.

Getting back to loving one another matters. I feel we have our differences and our comfort zones but in total awareness we flunked 'love' class. Simple reminders, then.

I wrote a few short books to help us to align us with our true nature. I have written poetry to help us along the lines of great beauty, likewise. Beauty is who we truly are 'within'. Hopefully some will poke at the poetry but truly it was presented to make one go deeply 'within' to quiet our noisy existence.

Peace be of us. (smile)

Life

Look at a seabed and fly to its moon
its reflection is borne of light. True beams,
of life above our head
illusive though it seems

to wave and roll on water crescents
in glistening whims near rolling rocks.
Bouncing bits of light silent, soundless
alive as a butterfly knocks

on drums of windful puffs of gale
love and loveless, true.
For beauty denotes a wave of love
kindered within you

to blow a tune so mystic
so great, it's waterfalls
that seem light in comparison
in beauty, their awe.

Talk in rain, snow, sleet if you must
life knows that already.
But talk of love as never known
nor seen makes the weary cheery

to love again or hold its hand
least we faint its absence.
Love is never gone from sight
in the heart of one, in innocence.

Loving what 'is' makes sense

No two ways about our Oneness

To date there are souls that would like to be first in every endeavor. This is true to one extent. On the other hand, these souls corrupt the entire gamut of the system of 'Oneness.' How is it that this is true on the one hand and on the other people who understand that the Universe is of One are not affected by this situation nor any other corruption?

Well, look around you. What do you see transpiring as Oneness? Basically when people fail to get in contact with the one place love abides which is 'within' then they are out of alignment with 'is-ness.' Anytime someone is being competitive or unreasoning when it comes to cooperation, there non-love is found.

Everyone wants peace. It's true we all have it to some extent today. Where is the love of good in nonsense that often accompanies the issue of 'Oneness' for the self analyst to discover we are all of peace, eventually? On the surface of matters, yes it is true that the Oneness we all possess is there operating in a sort of 'hum' along with the universe already.

Who hears its melody, though?

In this illustration we can feel the sun and its warmth on our soul as the body is the conduit that allows a person to be in contact with the divine. What happens when the person is left without the sun to feel its warmth? Life itself depends on such to see that all living beings are given a chance to survive.

In our society though, most are 'symbolically' without this source as love is too an essential essence element in which a soul thrives unlike a species that can inhabit a cold area due to its makeup. Otherwise, people want to be in charge of their lives and it's true they are to an extent.

But deep within there are forces that are in control, out of their reach. Some of these are our air supply, what we are aware of or otherwise needing such as our heartbeat or nervous system running effectively.

Many people are in fear of the unknown. Many hesitate when it comes to taking direction from another even if what is being expounded is 'wisdom itself.' The reason for this is because of our limited awareness as a species among our civilization. Those that inhabit our rainforest and of such areas, these are thought to be primitive in comparison to our city dwelling. Yet when these gentler civilizations that inhabit our many forest areas worldwide are encroached upon by our negative nature, they too began to experience what we consider normal but in reality hurt and harms their psyches as for most of them it is a permanent situation thrust upon them with no way out.

Their ability to survive is tantamount to living at peace with everything in creation including their social structures such as in a tribal setting. How is it people who dwell in cities are immune to those suffering? Could it be a lack of sensitivity? Sensitivity is needed in order to continue for us as a species to dwell on our planet. Many spiritual teachers have come to the aid of such issues. Many people too are waking up spiritually to a duty we have missed out on in the pass. But what of today and our future generation that is coming to the fore of humanity?

Certainly we all love having a good cry. What is life without an ability to get to the bottom of the issue for once? I myself love being able to write and expound on the message of 'Oneness.' Who today though cares about what happens to us as a species? Our senseless society is so busy in our breakneck pace of life we have little or no time for relaxation. It is such a pitiful waste of life. In places such as Hawaii or Bermuda these areas are beautiful and lovely.

Our entire planet is of such lovelessness if only we would stop first to think what we do now have to do with the future of our planet. Let's examine one such area.

Love calls for being kind. What can we change to become kind in an area that has not seen such? Females tend to be tender by nature, as well as nurtures and sweethearts to mankind among us.

Who would care to see that they are being treated kind and held worthy? So many females are under the gun. Who looks at their schedules and feels for their dissatisfaction? So much harm could be alleviated just on this one area among mankind itself.

Who would like to be kind to a baby? They are small, true. Yet, they suffer and are ignored under the weight of our constant busy society. When we are made aware that even infants in the womb being carried are affected to the same or greater degree as some Wall Street businessmen and their stress levels, who are we to say our need to evolve as a species is too slow?

Some may argue every letter in this publication as hearsay. On one level it may appear as though some societies are having a greater influence on our societies than any other ~ yet on another hand it may be construed being human and keeping current is everybody's problem.

What and where do these unborn children have if not us among the living to depend on for substance when they arrive among us? How is it we could forget the most peaceable among mankind? Are babies' culprits? Do they manipulate mankind? Are they unworthy of love from humanity as a whole?

Which baby, where? Any baby worldwide would concur. Premature babies are due to unnatural stress placed upon delicate umbilical cords even before they enter their third trimester in the womb.

What will lessen the ill effects upon a woman's body, then? The suffering among mankind then is avoidable, true? If we were to see a dog being mistreated there would be a society formed to prevent the mishap of the unconsciousness among mankind. Yet, so many of the unborn of our species too are in a similar position. They need our help. If it were your life in jeopardy you would want assistance so peace would be your lot.

Why do we hear less of a baby? Babies are our most fragile amidst our kind. Time is needed and patience ~ for their care is constant. But in our hurried, rushed pace everyone wants to be taken into consideration. How can this happen when the young among humankind are so unseeable, not given what is truly of worth, our attention? What of love, then? Children are sweet and worthy of our attention as a society in charge of their young.

Yet and still many just skirt right by them without so much as a 'I need you' or 'I want you, too' and not even a hug as most will content they feel uncomfortable speaking or tending to their sensitive youthful area for fear of being 'termed' too sissy-fied.

A cold demeanor then is sought after. So, everyone in tune with going 'within' are in need of a change of attitude, myself included. There have been times I too look at our women, children and infants and feel my schedule is too burdensome to attend to their fragile nature.

Being in our 'Oneness' mode for humanity will assist us to be kind in this area too for mankind is in just such a need of our attention. Whenever people scoff because they hate 'love,' that is due to their being selfish. Most will disagree. Let's look at this scenario again, though. Love will not look to its own needs first. It will bend to align itself with what '*is*.' So the mind doesn't get confused, what that is saying is put others ahead of your own convenience. Doing so makes for peace. Just the right touch of insistence and I'm sure we as a species will survive our most intimate issue at hand, peace as a way of being.

Love gives with the heart as joy is its counterpart.

When others in our keeping are left out of our affection, what transpires? Is it good to feel unloved? What of being alone with suffering and pain? Kinship has its privileges. When we are kin to kindness and being sensitive and loving what transpires? Wholeness, true?

What of being whole rather than fractured from being torn apart by the situation at present? Love ~ it's the answer, for who would want to suffer unjustly at the hands of a loved one be it their brother, sister or a family member?

It is remarkable to see people for once can come together in unity. Why wait for more injustice? Who wants it? We all have it to give but why bother with the latter?

Look at your hand. It is a tool of give and take. Which will you do for society at large or for just a simple assisted hand to see that a river, our air or a simple plant are kept safe from harm? There are those who do want to beat up so don't let it shock us. Where are you from anyway if you haven't noticed? That's what balance is. At least for once somebody's explaining it rather than hiding what matters of importance. If we had known this a while back I wouldn't even need to have to write this book. Our ignorance is mainly due to fear.

Want more truth? I need a break. Whoever is in charge of setting the bill prices, that's the person I'd like to leave this publication with first. So much life wasted on frivolous material aspirations with its 'me first' connotations I could just scream. I would like to live in a world with less monetary value placed on life unless it made for peace first. Like which came first, our bill system or life? Not proverbial, but I'd like to get a break in that area just the same. It's so relentless. (...whew, got that one off my chest too) Writing has become a vehicle for a realistic approach to solving what matters, for once. I see light at the end of the tunnel on this issue. If I get lots of fan mail, I'll be sure to cover the subject with earnest.

If people in the powers that be want a sincere approach to waste management, I'm here to talk. How many bullets equal justice for all humanity? Peace knows no such situation. Peace abides in love alone. Where did we veer off course? No time like the present to discuss money and care of the soul.

Once upon a time I use to be free. The wind knows it's true. Children are privy to this blessing, likewise. I do what I must to stay clear of most folly so as to stay attuned to what truly matters. Soul for soul, life thrives in Oneness alone. A soul in love with a day despite its madness is the way to not only be at peace but also it's in line with being realistic. I love my life. Trials come less often. Life is lighter. When I walk or drive down a lone country road (...as I live out in some of the most beautiful farm land in the country, southern Texas. They say everything is bigger here, it's true) my mind reverts to when I was young and lived in the city. I miss the hustle and bustle to a point but what I really love about me now is I'm in harmony with life. The country affords what the quiet city life could never give a soul.

Being One with the land and with nature is easiest out in an open field as oppose to a city park. Rarely does a human interfere with nature here.

What price have we put on our heart and our earth though she sustains us for free? Would you accept a check of any amount for your eyes? Of course not, they are priceless to you. It's the same with the way we are exterminating our water supply. Its use is immeasurable too but when we clamor that anything heaped upon our species or our planet or even our water supplies...well, is it not true that they too can reap upon our area what has been inundated upon their innocence such as nothing good nor pure to be given in return for us as a use for its soul?

A kitten, look at its innocence. We are that in our true mode of existence. But away from our wholeness 'Oneness' we forget that. A simple reminder will do mankind.

Why waste life unnecessarily whether its love or a resource. Both are areas under our control, then. Who comforts the poor and the weak among us? Some will say in God's good time everything will happen for the better. This is under scrutiny as I'm speaking so no explanation's needed. "Time is the cure, then," say most. Time is the one thing we use and it's been long past being improved upon in our lives let alone the planet, our area to keep alive by our deeds. Snuffing out life is at the fore as I speak.

Let's take a look at the deeds, shall we? One plus one equals one in One mode. Shift our attention to our deeds for NOW is of timelessness, our infinite peace resides within its sphere. NOW is whole, wholeness. There's only one humanity. We're fractured, though. Harm any one thing, everybody gets the result, see? If you don't like the math, do it right this time. Reality is not partial to ignorance. It's absorbed into Oneness, no-thingness with no return as all else but love, as love is its nature to any or all movement ~ be it good or evil. If I need to shut up about reality, it'll happen. Blessed be you, then.

If love is the issue pushed by humanity from every angle then sure love will transpire, true? The same with being insensitive or being among only those we feel are appropriate by individual society's norms.

To open up our hearts calls into question motive for who would be as unconditional as God? Man may argue, "If I'm good to everybody this time around then what's in it for me?" questions his old 'something for nothing' mode. Of course we can go down the already trotted issue of love who, when and where again. Love is the issue being expounded. Let's take a closer look at the eye of a bewildered society concerning the matter of love.

Love has to do with the 'inside' what some consider being of a sensitive nature. Going 'within' counts plenty as many are doing to date. These lovely folks harm no one. Just not enough in their group yet to make a significant difference for us as a whole. Sensitive people care about life. Just this one area alone baffles the mind in another. Even now it boggles the mind of those selfish among mankind why there are some who would actually go with genuine love. For what it's worth, these people are also loved too in return without measure. So who's to say what comes around goes around doesn't work? Love is flawless. Take a good look, love is operating just being stuffed, smothered or otherwise ignored at the price at times of others but mostly given to a loving being ~ love works. If given some other way for their being to operate, these kind ones wouldn't choose it for they like the way of the One. This is The Way…to operate as love being the premise for all not just some anymore, true?

There is a huge issue which can be satisfied if only given up to scrutiny, "Is life worth living today?" Under satisfying conditions of course life is worth living. Yet and still many today are suffering from enormous pressure to 'get the job done.' Who and where are these rules origin from?

If the origin is of mankind, then that makes the answer that much more easily to be handled ~ for there are not missing those that can give a help in the direction of supporting itself. Brain surgery is for surgeons. Do not have a procedure unless you feel the surgeon in question is competent to perform its duty. It's your soul. Use your commonsense, please. I write what I know of, love. Any takers who might want to choose hate? Again, for the sake of clarity ~ do your best, love will follow. For some, patience is the key.

When life is at stake as such a situation has arrived for mankind, in faltering where love is concerned then it's time for a new way of 'being' for it is about us being true in our nature as caring people.

'Being' is first. Being is of 'Oneness.' Its source is true, for it is divine also sacred in nature. Love is who we are as a species and we are of its wholeness, true? Would you like to play a game of "Let's see if humanity wakes up when everything is speaking, "Hey, I'm hurting!" spiritually speaking that is?

Love is a game to many. As any battle fought, there are its winners and losers with scars and scuffs as proof. Love has no such forum. Hatred though, bears a sense of "win at all cost so the sucker who truly loves gets to be society's losers."

Growing up with a sense of maturity like evolving with creation with movement at the fore calls for a change in outlook. Change with status quo is an oxymoron. Change makes us whole alone. Status quo believers, leave your ego at the 'please pass' sign so you can catch up with us who like life whole. Our self-serving mode has lived out its usefulness. Thank you, I know some of you will even be sweet about it.

Simple eloquence dictates please, inform us of our duty to our society as we are such in need of true direction. Truth? So, be it then. I write about love because I have had it up to my neck with people who have made me suffer for no other reason than they got the better of my good.

Good is a commodity to some. I feel abandoned, too. And I'm sure there are lots and plenty of folks that will agree with me.

My heart aches. I feel in Oneness alone. There are many like me around our spherical planet who can address their issue as a testament I'm not alone in this situation. If you love and I do ~ well, probably you'll like what's transpired in spite of the nay-sayers against peace returning, let alone love as I have.

I've chosen to speak, you may decide to agree in silence. I choose the road less traveled for the sake of my 3 children having just grown into young adults and fear they may be harmed if I keep silent about our worsening spiritual attire.

Wearing a badge of indifference has seen its day, so I thought, but that's another book. A long one, too. I like love. Enough said.

It's because people who love complain less. They have the greater satisfaction 'within'. To these, life is satisfying. When we love those that matter to us…these souls are as babies that are carried or children under our care. That's how we win in our humanity and our innocence resurfaces. So many times I have felt abandoned and left alone for no other reason than people felt I was already a positive, non-antagonistic, happy easy-going person so why not dump on me? And dump they did…loads! The formula is multiplied by tens of millions of other folks like myself, I'm sure.

With wisdom at the helm, this cannot transpire.

When a person is being loving or sweet as my children have become, would it be too much to ask for cooperation? Love is of such qualities. I have been hounded, scoffed and scorned for this beautiful quality. Is it right for anyone to have to experience such a demise let alone this new generation of our young among us to have to experience yet another generation of such like conduct with little recourse? I walked life sad and burdened and harmed. Should the children of our planet feel this yet one more generation? To what end? My sadness and grief was expounded knowing there are actually people who calculate the pain as a 'win' situation for humanity. It looked like basic immaturity, to be honest.

Yet is love not from above, divine even? We all are divine beings as we all posses love. Unity of humanity is of just such a quality. What are we waiting for? What bomb needs to drop on us to deliver us from the depth of human suffering? I have children as we all generally do. Our next generation then…harsh or kind? The future is ours to repair along with any soul that concerns themselves too, with kindness our attire.

Aligning ourselves with what works is the answer. Simple, love for humanity is a must, then. Is 'Oneness' and unity for our species a new gimmick to try on or a passing fad? Be in the moment and see how quickly we dispute with fear as our guide. Love has its privileges. A clean, beautified planet for one. Our sanity for another. And just the good old-fashion saying among us again, "Peace be with you." All highly evolved societies blessed another when greeted as endings were unheard of. As love would suffice, so too our planet is in need of it but more fully, though. What, where and how is it that the planet too is of its One or Oneness with us at the helm still unconscious yet evolving.

Let's expound.

Endurance for those kind among us makes sense to some people. For lack of a better word I'll call god, our highest personage or what have us midst humanity to call as such lord 'IT' as all is inclusive without lack. This calls into issue for the sake of argument what role god 'IT' plays when the entire world is going into a 'hellhole' so some retort.

This is an easy question to anyone who is aware and fully alive to the present issue which is under discussion, divine cooperation and such. Let's take a look at the air in which all living matter is 'supposedly' breathing.

In the end most will understand the issue from the standpoint of their mind which plays so little a function on the entire gamut of the universal issue of what is 'to be'. It's like who gets to keep the planet when at the point of physical death exposes its true nature, right? We're temporary at best. When the moment of truth finally arrives for these folks the issue and every or any other matter that has sufficed will be moot. So, who is to say?

Where is contradiction or issue at fault, the planet? Absolutely not, for at the day of a soul when it expires does not count where the whole of humanity is at stake or whether people will survive or even if the air supply is of adequate sufficiency. Laugh then, because the issue is temporary which includes thoughts that are irrelevant.

It's silly to try to be a One with all that encompasses its stealth mode which in some societies is considered a Great Mystery, true? Life is unknowable to the common person. This is as it should happen. This is just one of the easy matters that confront the human mind though from the standpoint of the 'above realm' Universal Consciousness we'll call it, this greater illumination starts only and just so that people will at some point accept the message that we too are included into the factor meaning in laymen's terms 'the divine suffices alone.' *IT* does its job complete and whole all the time not just Tuesday or tonight.

The above realm which consists of higher incarnations of existence still and always play a greater part in our existence. Whole up there (divine/heaven/upward) and fractured (people/earth/downward).

Intelligence is bread and grown on the earth to assist humanity and the world from the standpoint of its own matters at hand. Some may feel an urgent need to cooperate with the physical matters at hand first as oppose to getting in contact and resurfacing with a deeper wisdom which only in divine mode can it be received in any sufficient quality.

Living a physical only surface, superficial existence is certainly full of fun. Many do love life as 'is' and complain rarely. Of course there are those at the extreme end of that equation that would love to be included and since they are, we will discuss how, where and when their dissatisfaction arises from.

Whenever a soul is not happy or satisfied with the immediate situation facing them, they usually tend to go into the mind mode only to the exclusion of the soul excluding from themselves for whatever reason the deeper issue that can only be sufficient when gathered from 'within' called peace. Peace is *Wisdom Incarnate*. The mind has no such surface to phantom an incorruptible attire of love which is useful yet plentiful as 'It' is, most will dismiss It's love as not the answer. Again, for the sake of reiteration – the mind is temporary and not in the correct place when the truth comes knocking.

Let's suppose we all for Its sake did come from love, our deepest asset. What would love produce besides the usual answer, that we would be nice to one another the whole world over even and including the soul itself, you? People complain out of fear. There are truly only two recourses in which the entire issue hangs upon – fear or love. There is just these two. There is no such in-between. Go and stop. If we pause or think about love rather than move with it as compassion, empathy or being sympathetic and not close our ears to those in need, then of course we're divine. We're 'go'. Not a bad idea. Could happen in theory. One suffices 'all knowing' to Itself so 'stop' is within its jurisdiction, too. Otherwise a dumb universe where the shore has no bounds nor equal sunlight to evening. The vernal equinox is of intelligent design as in – no heaven, no earth. Since we have an earth, it suffices the spirit is alive without our participation for want is not needed nor heard of there.

So, what is One to consider if pain, suffering or even death were to transpire before our soul to be taken into consideration at the blessed event as all such incidents are just that. To those who are awakened fully to their true nature as being of love alone – heaven assist so as not to 'bottom out' on you guys. Great math for the weary, some losers with their selfish mode needing a good upheaval from the helm of society least we 'bottom out' on our fun time for to not be pestered 'til death do us part' is sufficient for all, yes?

So let's start anew never. That's what transpires when a conscious society awakens from its stupor with the superficial thought that everything ends as oppose to the truth, in reality everything is alive. If and when a transference of *consciousness* in the spirit within comes to the fore – then humanity will of course see the need for change to be at the helm, for truly no better blessed words have transpired then when they were spoken, "You will be with me in paradise." This book is that passage incarnate. Wisdom has its knowing from above only. Sense it in your soul. See it as wisdom returned, also.

What paradise, where even when? This is the crux due to plea. Life at an apparent worst event still sticks to what works, being positive and true to its nature to call into existence the One intelligence. The divine truth of love is never absent from any situation. Where and when do you feel it most that what will happen next is still of divine awareness? Always, I hope. Even if people are less evolved and think love doesn't exist, still there love is in all its blaring glory for your nice tush to wake the bless up! Sigh. (...a moment to recant my patient nature, then.)

In the hopes of disassembling a situation which the mind does called ego, at best then when it does separate one from the source of love Itself then the 'above' is considered not functioning or has dismissed Itself from observing our low periods when they happen upon us. In our own disillusionment then, fear comes into play and the entire situation turns out not as pleasant as we would have hoped. Love fights no one. Even when provoked, most that are pleasant of any degree better their chances oppose to those that are always in the right and willing to accept a non-conformity of the divine to take the situation instead. This meaning love is present and eternally here and ones who are not privy to its blessing is due to being (...against such to happen, don't want it here ever and mostly hate love for it has components that will loosen its bearing of being right as oppose to cooperating with others they see as inferior or less worthy then their soul) not in control of the place but want to. So, I'll say it once more. A selfless attire, please.

Some have a superior complex and others have an inferior complex. Either or will stifle love in oneself and another. So maturity ~ take a bow today for joining our rakes of the sane among us.

Let's take a look at Colonel Powell in the position that makes the most elaborate celebration of life to those who are in need of his command. When and how did those who were under his leadership respond to his guidance? Was there dissention or a being at war with his decision as best to conserve peace through negation first, as most do follow this course.

Of course, for his troops to listen they excelled in their attempt to get to issues rather than bear arms. In the larger scheme of matters this is what truly transpires. War of course happens but to judge harshly any event is the beginning of a failed relationship with the truth of the situation. Do we know the result? Did we need to? Who gets to have the final say? Above then, it's the only recourse to take when given a choice. Go with the situation that transpires. What if you don't want to? Ask Colonel Powell first. His word is moot and so too whatever transpires thereof. So listen to reality, it helps.

Is there someone who could use help?

That is there, also. And true to nature of a loving soul the one in need will certainly be the recipient of your generous action. Love the way you want to be loved, then.

Let's examine hope from an all encompassing viewpoint rather than from our earthly standpoint alone. Hope is a by-product of peace, true? Truth also matters as any realistic situation encompassing the divine would transpose for the sake of knowing what is true for One.

Hope is not a selfish but rather a selfless pursuit of happiness. Where selfishness rears its petty head people suffer ignominiously due to again their limited unknowable stance of not knowing the only oblivious outcome, failure and defeat in magnitude proportions. For who wants to suffer in dumb anguish as oppose to being free to be alive in the moment with happiness and good that accompany the other choice that could have been taken, to love?

Choice is otherworldly like love and peace are. "Who says?" asks a temporary mind movement of thought out there as surely as rain, air and snow exist among mankind. Bravery is suitable for those who love without fear. At the end of the opposite polarity of existence in form there are the 'no' sayers indeed. When confronted with their ego to rant and rave for a better tomorrow with the exclusion of love, the only answer that works best from the standpoint of those that are also present in the divine, would it not be better to choose this recourse?

For so long, people who were caring were so discounted. Besides being a joke otherwise known as unconsciousness ~ what happens transpires due to love being not chosen. In our atmosphere, for people who love and are sincerely loving this must be an eye opening situation. "We are at choice?" some will ask themselves I'm sure. Why of course! Every human is able to do what makes sense, even being unlikeable. What is cherished to one, at the other end of the spectrum are those that have a more then average dislike, deathlike even disposition for the same object or person in question.

What to do? For those who like (...whatever) stay clear of those that outwardly hate and oppose your obvious truth, that you like it. Why? Never mind that.

Try an experiment. Leave what you say out there. If the person still disagrees then for the sake of argument and an unpleasant circumstance to rear ~ leave or walk away. Certainly there are things too, that the disagreeable person likes that you have in common with it also, true? For in the universal sense of using "common sense" (which is sorely not functioning today in our spiritual absent condition) mankind has walked themselves into that area. Just be true and trusting as love would have it.

To argue an absolute is futile. Its pain worthy experience is trustworthy enough. Some have had it with the non-sense and come to their senses and a 'spiritual awakening' and it happens when and where we least expect growth from ~ our soul or that of another.

Like illness for example. Some use it to grow and see what will become of the situation in a positive assertive manner while others rant and rave that life is unfair although every other human experiences being sick at one point or another the situation to an unconscious individual will only conclude war to extinguish the 'bug' causing the illness as oppose to being spiritually aware that a universal truth holds to without prejudice.

The same holds true for wealth, beauty or any other human endeavor. Corresponding to the theme of love then, let's hold true to the reality of love with choice being a factor in whether we wake up in our spirit or falter. But then, "Who again is at fault?" as some would question even this in their unenlightened mode of which humanity functions.

Here's a thought....where the obvious participant in an untimely event is being peaceful, let that person have its way if only for once, please.

I'll beg if I have to.

The old mode of 'might makes right' then is replaced with a bigger concern at humanity's feet in which we as a species are facing. Accept society 'as they are' will hit a cord for some. They will question the sanity and the worthiness of infinite wisdom to be of One and love what 'is' transpiring as oppose to getting involved with a fruitless endeavor like arguing for the sake of peace. The oxymoron of being at peace with war suffices then, due to age and its inexperience. Where life concerns matter to us and even truth, the loveless state of humanity being at the center of the storm as oppose to the outer circumstance of what transpires where future is called into play or will at least for those who understand that being kind will only suffice NOW as oppose to the non-sense of yesterday, year and the following of what makes for a universal wholeness, us.

Yes, us.

This meaning not holding one gender to be a 'thing' again. No-thing or thing. Choose. It's one or the other this time around. Everything is alive in breathless One. Divine beings are cute, for they are kittens and poofy clouds being childlike in nature and definitely playful and full of life. Please, do not squash their awareness into a 'box' of linear disillusionment for the sake of being 'right' and the old 'might makes right.' Instead, be like these qualities ~ try softer elements of humanity such as gentleness or flexibility in its warmth as oppose to a cool nature with its cold demeanor. Love exists to the exclusion of the latter.

Love is unheard due to an absence of 'being' called silly. Loving beings are not silly creatures at all! Loving life is the beauty, so why harm a soul in its merriment?

Wisdom is innate in our youth. Where did it go ~ the easy nature to laugh, play and otherwise? Know that life is full of adventure and exploration!

Revert to a childlike nature, then. What is lost is worthy. Pick up not a gun but rather a pruning shear. The solution to care is in our hands as choice is otherworldly as any other miracle that exists that transforms a situation from ungodly unacceptable to goodness. Universal Consciousness or love is at peace with love more than war ~ is this true or false? Love is true, for it stands forever and withstands war. So do the math. Love is equationless and not to be known. Asking a man to understand a woman comes close to reality as such is unknowable at best. The down side (or up) is women know themselves perfectly ~ meaning they are in an excellent position to explain what 'coming from within' can mean from their perspective, too. The crux due to plea as a male and a blessing is his female counterpart.

A universal understanding of peace is obvious from the stand point where '*feelings*' come into play as a certain innate sensitivity with its by-product in One. Whole for those in their fractured ego attire – huh... ahmmm. Thinking is required true but in its unenlightened, unevolved state the answer is obvious that '*feelings*' are our greater truth. First see how you feel about a matter then move in the direction as love would have you.

Who is brave enough to feel love full force? Babies win, they come in whole and unadulterated by society as do kittens and lambs. All things new then are to be the ones to assist us in our evolvement as innocent creatures as those who will to bend would have it.

For lack of a better work I get disconcerted concerning a wavelength otherwise

known as the human species. For example, let's take football pro Troy Aikman stealth with a football. Are we to blame the universe, God (as some would have you) because he possesses everything a woman would die for? Who chooses who becomes the athlete pro, our next president or what have you? Are we here for a purpose?

Let's say there was no such thing as a Troy Aikman super hero to most.

Perish the thought I know yet we all have one thing in common with all else ~ we live, we

procreate (at least most have) and we move on. Looks simple from below. Above though, even this is carefully seen to as balance such as "Hey look, that one can't toss that darn ball! What gives?" must take place. So, be it super athlete or one without an ounce of athletic ability let's accept our Oneness as such is arguementless. A good coach could help the latter besides so let's get busy and whom ever cares to seek assistance from another for what have you, let's be more accepting this go round.

Love is whole ~ One

Islands love her waves, assured
shells adorn her body.
Life's abreeze come June nor September
whence love's ignored. A dove key

borne of love as all know
its merrier come June,
lessons learned in love means learning
June is One on noon.

Bright's her star in the sky
Cirrus her melody,
melancholy a moment in two,
an atom split softly

for anyone, anywhere, anytime
to see love in action.
How's it for love to come calling?
Like weight lifted knowin'

we caused a rift, glory caused.
Put out our light, our love.
For love of anything is due now.
Bewinged midst love's return, its dove.

Harmony

Everybody love a winner

The beauty of our differences transposes as our being at odds with each other which is sweet to the touch of One. For the human it's anything but. In wisdom I'm formed to delight so One wins. One / won ~ see how it works? Notwithstanding our pride, preferences and judgments we can keep our soul alive where it comes to interacting with one another again.

When One transposes Itself from two where humanity is heading so love once again is at the helm ~ instead of us being human, we'll suffice ourselves/souls with love as never could thought, do nor thinking as a by-product of an over-active mind in its unevolved, unconscious, limiting state could ever have delivered us from.

To ignore another when in need is liken to the planets colliding with one another for the sake of speed. Too much ego does the same thing and what a disaster, too! (…ego refers to separation) But when we One our planet, even such luminaries as a nebula or a wormhole or a galaxy takes notice due to our transformation in awareness. Where love prevails our souls connect again in an alignment with all in existence as we are all One indeed including our solar system. The Milky Way entertains itself at our behalf. Twinkly, starry and in beautiful alignment with our inwardly stealth yet feasibly made adorned attire meaning us as humanity being 'wisdom incarnate' once more.

Time wise, wisdom is infinite. And true to being itself, the universe becomes once again in love with our existence for in our unevolved state our planet was loud and unruly still.

What is 'truth'? The question holds a mystery like who shot Kennedy or more like water as oppose to wine. It's a preference, like flowers. Some swear by their love as a token of affection while others would pass on their sentiment with its meaning, saying in jest, "No thanks, war is tastier than peace." Brute force comes into play for our planet is so steeped and unaligned with wisdom it reeks as a joke for those unenlightened to their obvious worth and beauty. It's true that dense, selfish or unruly people are a part of reality. Accept it as a 'whole experience,' though. The opposite polarity of life is just that. No fog in One anymore, love is crystal clear Now humanity as oppose to giving a bit course over a full meal.

Now I'm sure there will be some minds out there refusing this moment as peace. Therefore allow me to introduce you to the most perfect person that can assist one to perfection, myself included. That would be humanity. "Hold it!" some will say loud enough to maybe be right again although right is relative to wrong, while in absolute neither exist otherwise we'd all be gunk of the universe ~ asteroids and such.

We all have within what we call 'Consciousness'. When people are aware in this mode ~ only then we all are perceived as the literal and symbolic Garden of Eden. This garden metaphorically exists 'within'. As more people attune themselves to this area of inner knowing, the chances of our outer existence too will follow, thus a return to a literal paradise here on earth.

I am here to assist us to be of One again and in the end it will happen just as soon as we decide that being unattended to the earth no longer suffices. Plant a tree, get familiar with a seed. Allow growth of the planet again so we all achieve a place of love not just our own species.

Include the entire gamut of life itself again and wisdom will deliver us from this place of being amiss with Oneness still a part of our activities, again.

Being divine in nature for the purpose of finally getting to the crux of the problem that has had its nasty hand on mankind has been lifting so that the entire gamut of the universe will finally get to the fun of their own life. This means whales swim again in our oceans without mishap at our hands or birds fly free without sudden shifts in our air currents to misguide their flying patterns come season change and even a boat would not be in fear of a sudden shift in water currents to up-heave its vessel without moment's notice as such transpires under our careless endeavor to chart our 'waters of life' in directions unknown by nature.

Please see this book as only a part of the issue that will assist in getting humans to get the way of the whale - fun, alive and just swimming around just for the reason of its divine purpose alone, loving the day.

Does that sound fun, funny even? Who wants it? Who could accrue to the majesty of loving every moment of life when even a beaver in the river or a tree or a kitten loves existence no less then we do?

Why is humanity so slow to just be happy within existence as all the other forms in existence is just as busy but not coincidentally opposed to the blessing of this life? The moment is true to Itself.

Here's a solution, a pair of antelope one male the other female. Where then is the source of its being? Is it in business holding practices against its better judgment despite knowing better or maybe shopping for another hoof to adorn its pride or perhaps maybe swimming in a lather of mud to escape the unwarranted heat with the exasperation that accompanies over exertion due to fatigue of being overburdened with worry for tomorrows stock tip? We'll just purport their side for once to see what it looks like from their viewpoint. Does it look silly yet? Have we had enough?

Please for the sake of getting to the part where love plays its role, let's do what makes sense for once. Beauty is a by-product of peace. As a wheel with spokes in them, every facet of life has its beauty revealed within as without. But where their takers? It's nice to be in their presence, flowers that is - but where the patience to accompany their sole purpose for being?

Please, be patient with me. I'm exasperated due to wanting to understand the nature of life, also. I'm perplexed beyond limit at times. Let's say for what-if purposes women could chant a hymn that would get a male to actually like their presence as oppose their meetings in their opposite condition to oneself.

Beauty would dictate what love would suppose happen. Here for the sake of balance within our up/down in/out yes/no forces at work, suppose a male was sensitive to the needs of his female counterpart rather then his own at the fore? What would transpire where love failed previously ~ for humanity is in such a wreck to get on with something other then being humane with its dried-out bone scenario that if true substance were the prize, would it not be fair to humanity to at least consider the option?

"Beauty is a luxury," some purport. Not true, least we all be deficient of its character which is not able to happen ever. Due to its formlessness meaning, it's here in infinite always anyhow. So saying that, what's truly missing is our being present to beauty's worth and possibly even wanting to rid oneself of old worn-out modes of conduct that would damage a female ~ for outwardly she'll remain silent for fear of retribution.

"Love will have its way with us then!" some will sigh. And with good reason ~ for selfishness has reared its ability to close down the shop to enlighten our souls for all time, not just now but for future generations to stall in growth with the rest of creation.

Love has a momentum and humanity's the slowest to achieve harmony whereby all other creatures in creation are peaceably co-existing for the betterment of balance. We are out of alignment with love Itself. Look at a turtle. "Slow," many will reply. Who won the race, though? Patience is its virtue? No, its character is being true unlike the rabbit who fast-paced itself out of the game, fast asleep without a care. Sounds like humans on their fast track to me and out of whack with everything whole.

What harmony is there in being mean or cruel ~ destructive, even? Give yourself the expression of the peace that is you. It's there everywhere! What are we all as a species waiting for?

You are missing the fun! How is the gamut of the entire universe to be truly in harmony when even a duck can swim in peace? Does that sound strange? Are they at war? When? Where? Are they being cruel beyond understand? Are their temporary mishaps senseless? Of course not! Though they are territorial, they swim in flux due to a season of not being at peace, true but shortly thereafter they'll assist one another as though the incidence never occurred. Being human we have a tendency to hold grudges, (dear lord...)

In other words ~ no harmony, no peace. Rules abide by themselves another way of saying a boom-a-rang can't do its job because it'll slitter on the ground because 'we' couldn't catch the blessed flying object ~ so over our head it flew by us! Won't stop it from being a boom-a-rang, though! This is the only person to be able to confer this kind of transference of love, you. We have a say humanity, did you not know this? You need to know the rules to grow up, be mature or at least get it right for once where love matters.

As far as the entire world of humanity being in a lost situation as far as love concerns itself, anyone can be nice to another. (...a moment of silence. Cricket, cricket. I'm still reeling why love is absent here, Now.) The solution is moot, then. There goes the end of war, shouting, pushing and all its foolishness that encompasses selfishness at the helm. Love besides not looking to its own interest is the key or another way of saying 'kindness' makes for a future worthy of our being a part of something wonderful, great and grand ~ life amidst creation! And good ~ don't forget that one! Good is here to stay.

People today are always working on one project or another. This is good to a point. On the other, many people would love to have as much of love for themselves as though it is going to disappear somehow. This is the illusion not the reality of the situation. Love is endless so why grasp at it as though it's limited in any form whatsoever?

Most people accept help when needed. What of the sun? Is it in need of anything in particular? "Why bother with the other side of the issue that does not affect you?" some may ask.

Well, the sun does have a need. "What could that be?" you may ask in earnest since we all cannot affect its performance. No, not true. We do affect the sector of our solar system as a species.

The sun uses our rays that are bounced off our planet and emitted into our atmosphere and beyond our galaxy in a flux situation. You as the sun would want to speak of the unlikely situation of being effectionless as the fallacy it is in truth. Why hurt the sun? Why is it hurting? Because of our ignorance, that's why! What if children in grade schools were educated for once by an enlightened person who understands that mankind is opposed to being nice to even its outer alignment of its species?

What balance, indeed! We are connected to the universe. We need to be open to its correction. If the sun does retaliate in its wisdom to correct our situation, what of our higher purpose to get to the crux of our existence, then?

What about meat consumption out of balance on our planet? Do you feel it does not affect the atmosphere this way or the other? It does by the over farming it produces.

People love the earth. Why would anyone want to leave a planet behind to a later generation torn and bruised and mismanaged? What of the air we breathe?

Look at the leaves come autumn when they land softly on the planet. Did the wind kick them around or were they gently tossed in a playful atmosphere where once again they were whirled and twirled into a giddy existence ~ for their being is soft of nature. The wind is aware, are we? As a species what is it to wake up to a spiritual One as oppose to a 'two' existence meaning coming from our physical existence alone. Sense your atmosphere. Feel life brimming. It needs nothing.

Just let it be.

If the wind were to change into a person, she would appreciate it if she were treated with dignity, respect and comforted as though she were wise ~ for true to her nature she is. Have you not seen her currents? She blows in uniform and she's got it made! She doesn't antagonize people with her power and might though she should. Heck, why not? People are supposedly sane. If she were to go off course as we do so under the guise of being 'cleverly more intelligent' because she's just an abstract 'thing' ~ would it be fair to call her awful or a stupid breeze we're having today? I think you know what's happening here but just the same, why do you suppose people are so slow to want change to be nice to her? She likes us otherwise we'd be blown out of the atmosphere due to her might force gale. Think it can't happen? Tsunamis are currents and are One as any current of wind power for power. That being true, a similar scenario as probable could develop should mismanagement continue from our sector.

Is ugly in fashion? What is the matter with people the world over that they cannot see what they are doing to the night stars, our galaxy or the moon, even?

Be in the moment for once for it is forever which it is truly when we're in One mode. Do we want to get better? "No, I'd rather stay the same," most will retort. "Convenience has its privileges," they smile although nature watches our smug retort in wise mysticism.

"With change comes inconvenience," some mutter distraughtly. Nobody wants that, (...lord knows) yet we chaff under the weight of our existence as though being wiser then nature would call for is the ticket to living in blessed harmony with her. Love is different then you and me in what is called 'normal'. Our everyday existence is manifested as non-sufficient. "If bank lingo were the terminology we'd use to express our dissatisfaction with basic human activity," said the whale "as though beavers of our riverbanks or moose of our meadows were missing legitimate deposit slips in our bank of life together, remember them?" asks the whale in concern for mankind's indifference toward their wildlife.

Moose don't want to hoof around our shopping malls, neither. (I figured I'd just throw that in there.) Can we discount the present condition to another generation to do the work our generation purports to abandon? It's not fair, they are younger. We who lead our youth are up in age and experienced and the young must abide by our standard for we are (gulp) wiser.

As I mentioned before the moon and the sun are just a little fed up. Not enough to function off course to affect our survival or continuation of our species...yet.

The moon and the sun live on a rotation that depends on the beams that shot off their surface as they emit rays that are needed to keep them on their planetary route. When the delicate balance of the universe is suffering because humanity does not feel the pain it incurs in another location, it makes for foul play none-the-less.

Who wants to be the moon today? Can you feel her bruises coming through the solar system as dust that bites and harms the rest of the residue that is suppose to be in her atmosphere but yet now absent as any extinct species among humanity's care? Just because they don't teach these sciences in the classroom they are likened to the experimental animals that have suffered for nothing better than to exploration of nothing of great value to neither our solar system nor to humanity. So what if another species is harmed? Let me expound to humans what it feels like to be a mouse today.

As a mouse, they like to squeak and squeal and run about. Do most people see a comparison with that of a child in existence because they should. But because they are smaller then us and want to be in existence just for the sole purpose of being alive and happy to live, most people will discount them as nasty or unnecessary. But balance in nature dictates we do not hurt or harm a hair on their head.

Instead live at peaceful harmony with their childish antics. Did they bite anyone lately? Have you a record they have unless needlessly attacked? Why give them a name, then such as 'dirty' or 'awful to be around' or worst yet harm it because it's wrong in being here? In our unenlightened ignorance we do these acts of unkindness. They are here to keep balance for us in nature, likewise the ant. Many step on them but they keep balance for our protection.

Who wants to be a puppy in our day and age? Most have no such life as they need. They are kept pets. Truly they are loved by humanity but is it true they need us for protection or is it the other way around? They are in no such need for man to protect anything of its soul.

They have a purpose and need beyond man's evolved situation. At least the puppies of the land are free. Man has yet to acknowledge this privilege for himself. Yes, in some countries there is a measure of what can be construed as freedom but really what is it in its truest form if not to be free from being imposed upon by a set of substandard living arrangements known only as society has profunctioned itself upon its personage.

If left in the wild, a dog of any species will see the light of creation upon its soul immediately. Who is the owner of the planet and the dog has been given such opposition to their management that even a dog if could be given the opportunity to speak as today they have would accrue to say, "Why am I not as precious as any other person, persons to date? I have fur, true. Yet, without my divine 'spark' to keep in existence, I too would not have the ability to 'be'."

Why is humanity so in a rush to exceed their limitation upon another creature in existence rather than the harmony and balance that's needed? It's there for the taking, our truth or fallacy of existence.

What of our supreme court? Who would trifle with the wisdom of running a country loved and dear to its soul? In love then, let us all cooperate with the powers that be ~ so harmony will ring in justice alone not just for our planet but for every creature in existence, as a nuisance all would be without a court of law to accrue for favor least we all be abandoned to wanton misconduct.

Why is the divine, what is sacred in society so in flux liken to being without its soul? As Oneness is accrued to throughout this entire theme, allow me to just say for the record that the rain and the wind are in need of one another. Why question the matter?

Yet and once again we are brought back to the role humanity is playing on it and its existence. First of all, every person on the plant is involved in playing a role today whether they are aware of it or not. Mostly 'not' due to the unconscious nature of the human family mainly in the area of love itself.

Let's look at the sunshine. Any takers? First of all its stronger than any person on the planet. What's the big deal with the sun being the only source that will give mankind what is the most important thing missing, true knowledge or its essence returned in wholeness once more?

People have very rarely been given the opportunity to talk to anyone that is enlightened to the point of absolution or completely of the divine. What of mankind's ascension to its main event, love?

Do you want to be a part of it, absent again or just fooling around the issue of love for the sake of observation while lesser more adept souls participate? At least that's what it appears to the mind. People who love are assisting humanity to peace itself. Is the job for them alone, I ask in earnest? No. How are we to conduct this matter at present so that everyone is taken into account? Mankind is supposing it's someone else out there as the old, "Let the other guy handle the situation" comes to the fore.

So, try not to do that again. It's a stall to enlightened beings that have amassed to assist humanity in its spiritual awakening. Peace can conform to a suggestion as well as to a demand.

As much as these teachers at present that teach along the lines of love are concerned, everyone is to listen to God. It's our truest nature as well as an error in what consciousness is accruing to help us to wake up to our spiritual responsibility as a species. We are at choice. Pick or chose folly or wisdom to be our guide.

We make the mess. Who is held accountable? The higher powers? No, allow humans to see that consequence plays her hand. If you want out of the mess we have put here to date, than make the choice to a higher power ~ meaning love itself.

I have a key to open knowledge not given for people are waiting to be awakened from its stupor of inactivity where love is concerned. Who keeps up matters little to anyone in particular. From one perspective people feel I'm an enlightened soul and from another perspective I'm really not because I'm a student being One with the whole of creation and this moment being all that transpires, I don't really know the outcome any less than anyone else. We are It and life is transposing itself upon our person. I'm content to allow it to transpire in grace as should we all.

Love In Our Being is a choice we cannot afford to abandon. Feel assured as a species we can hit this mark without the error of 'time' getting our attention. Go with our 'timeless' selves ~ as only love will suffice to break millenniums of abuse we managed to get ourselves into.

Besides, even the planet says, "Wake up society!" to be our best we have to offer her. Be with the planet on this one mankind ~ know our planet as the only place we have to live out our souls. Where else can society make life happen?

There's a moment
to touch
a bee of desire,
to meet in the
center,
to be in its fire.

Love was missing in society

Why bother with being clueless?

Now is the time for the winds of change to take place so that every living thing in creation has a beautiful way to see life as it has now occurred. Many love our living spaces to be adorned for the beauty of life to be reflected in our homes.

And it's true that the beauty that life has to offer is timeless as oppose to the using of time alone to achieve what mankind has missed, themselves in harmonic Oneness of peace.

Women too have been overlooked from the standpoint of all that matters in the evolution of our species. Allow such to free themselves from 'time' and all it offers in the way of busyness and it's over burdeness to their souls. How many people truly assist their neighbor to carry a load they themselves see but due to the wanton disregard for another person or species get left out of what truly matters in our overall care of our species? What of all these children of our care? Do we want people of another race, religion or statusless people to get an equal footing?

Walk softly on the earth is being offered to humanity once more as oppose to the horseplay on a situation in need of our attention. If a forest were to speak, what would she bereft of her life sources bemoan to our wise ears among us, then? Would it not sound like "Please bless our area for the sake of its wildlife, their young and a safe passage for all who inhabit my area, too?" Life is a woven web of trust/distrusted, then. Our crossroads of change are upon us clearly enough Now.

We all feel we have little or no ability today to give in that one area that life bemoans our presence - being of compassionate attire. To those lowly and meek I am blessed and of good countenance, whereby to others in selfish mode their anthem is 'bring it on, girlie." I'm only 5 feet but the challenge has presented itself to our better judgment so the moment be of its best, here goes:

Get out of our forest with your hell if you don't care for unity of a tree with its counterpart, all of us as One in our existence on the planet we inhabit together side by side in a twisted give and take. Instead of taking in stupefied horror to her harm and her creatures that coexists in peace since you're oblivious to her good so the next generation will bless her with wisdom and nurture her wounded parcel and lot.

Okay that being said, (…whew!) what is lost if we all accept our situation to remain as it has been to date? Then, what change has taken place for the betterment where satisfaction of our lives as a whole species is concerned? Why not the other guy? When will he finally get it right?

The pointing finger concept will not do for everyone has been in the grip of sadness, profound unkindness and at this juncture of our evolution ask yourself if it is possible to bring about change in an atmosphere of disbelief as we need to do this for our own good among humanity.

Love is good and kind always where the compassionate care for our lowly planet, children and even our old among society concerns itself. Sure, it takes much patience on the part of us as a whole to step back and evaluate what matters to life itself, everyone not just a few chosen. We have been so inundated with the stuff that matters so little to anyone other than rob banks to get ahead, most will travel the road least traveled and leave the senselessness of all that life has been telling them what is right and good for everyone concerned and accept what most would consider stupid, unreasonable and cruel on our individual continental budget (money) allowances, instead.

What is wrong with this approach? The cause will certainly have its way on the effect of not only the planet but on the senses as well. Commonsense though useful in our road to recovery is rarely used. What money could be as important or lovely as a rainbow after a rain shower? Who looks at them anymore? Who looks at a river except in disgust? Wasn't the river's fault.

What do we do, then? Come back to our humanist. Love is it. This is simple yet effective to turn people for once to look outside the box (as cruel as it has been to them to date) and grow something on the planet (perhaps growing a garden) as oppose to destroying her abundance to sustain herself. Our planet needs her water supply ~ not just the animals and the plants and we humans. Who comes after our generation matters, true?

Are flowers our enemies? Are they at the helm of society ordering cruel unreasonable demands on the others in existence? Is it they (…as if the flowers are at fault.) that are doing the culprit activity that needs to be halted for the sake of another? Where is this atmosphere of lovelessness and total disregard for all life being breed and borne from, then?

Is this to say everyone is a culprit? How can that be? "Many are hardworking parents!" some retort. Grandparents are quite loving when they reach their grace. Many children are the ones suffering today. So let's look at the bulk of society that are at the helm making the decisions for our tomorrow.

Everyone, not just a few count and matter today. Love has everything to do with whatever station a person is holding . If you think the environment is going to be turned around over night, think again.

Time is the only solution. Give what must be of importance Now. The future is not happenstance neither will fairies nor hoping with its wishful thinking help us actuate the reality of love.

Children like fairytales. They feel that the only way to escape the reality of modern society is to act out in a way to have others pay attention. Whether it's unhealthy behavior or just playing around with drugs, guns or otherwise. These will never produce the love and acceptance of one another no matter how hard people try to escape their miserable circumstances.

Love was missing in every area that mattered most to the very young, our youth in our generation thru to our elderly of the most advanced ages among every civilization on earth. Civilized… (and I beg to differ.) Commonsense has a way of knowing what needs are to be met. Like our vanishing waterways so too these innocent parties are part and partial of the wholeness of what matters.

Today is a day of change. Change and status quo is up for grabs.

Today, tomorrow and into infinity choice effects the outcome at any given instance. For example, again ~ babies love company. If left for too long its emotion and mental facilities are permanently and irreparably damaged when love is absent. A nurturer with its care giving then, needs to hold, cuddle and rock these young infants of humanity. "It takes time and patience and an enormous amount of work!" some excuse themselves, again. And still say, "I'll pass on the delivery of mankind. Wholeness yes, sure I'm all for that and I hear it makes for peace, even" say some in indifference still.

So off we go to leave the little guy to exasperate itself under an empty hollowed out shell of existence. Substance for all, then. We win as a whole when the need is presented and met. We lose humanity when it is forsaken.

Accept what matters first to the whole being of society. Why change our direction so that everything in creation is looked upon as what is in need of love and our attention once or twice if we give a care. Because attention as oppose to our inattentive indifference is what got us here.

I have had many people come to me for readings in hypnotherapy. Readings are done on the ethereal level as oppose to taking only the physical part of our existence into account. Many people are ashamed when love is pointed to as the solution and that the culprit could be we ourselves. At first there is shock but most feel satisfied that the solution is still the champion of all issue everywhere, love itself.

What's in it for humanity when we are all on the same page? Does that mean the higher powers to date were indifferent to our situation be it of divine origin or of man himself?

No, humans need time and even that is a conundrum. What of dentist, doctors or others of very high and astute nature when society awakens from its stupor in its loveless absent attire? These services are still operating for the efficient use in our society as a whole. What of our teachers and educators, law enforcement agencies of every kind and worldwide judges of every court? And even what is it of our business sector to accrue to love and change for the satisfaction of all under their care and guidance?

Yes, it is true. Love can rear her beauty in the way of being fair and in assisting others even in these capacities. Will love rule, though? What will it take to do so? Who gets glory's lot and power when the elite all over the planet are finally seeing the light at the end of the tunnel?

Well, the truth is love and her beauty is forever reigning as it should on its throne on a daily basis. All we have to do is accept its grace of kindness and forward it to those next in line of its reward to be felt rather than stunted from growth. Change. We all need it. It's here for the taking.

Change is here for the taking. I did, I use to be a maid. It's what I did for a living. That's how I met my dear friend Miss Penny we all use to call her. One of the most giving people still left on the planet. Self-made millionaire, that one. She entrusted me with her every move. There's freedom in true friendship. She owns two estates one where she owns home and lot to an entire mountain top view yet I felt humbled in her patience with my short comings on many issues of life. I cried when I left her employment. She's good with staff having being reared by her parents with over 30 servants at beck and call she understands the needs of the lowly. She's from India and has witnessed more than anyone of what's considered our unconsciousness where poverty of spirit and material needs could be more to our heartfelt forefront where our nature could hold a trust in loving home or society.

She has known the likes of beauty only few can imagine. A wealthy father who ran his own business to the tune of the family being among the wealthiest of families in their day.

Yet, when I first met her you could never tell. I fell instantly in love with her all too open and trusting nature. Heaven only knows why she can be so open. Like an untouched oasis. She never married but befriended so many people along her journey. She lends without interest, her model being "Love has her back so what could go wrong?" It's gotten her in quite a few financial mishaps to a soul or two who would not pay in earnest what was given from a pure motive.

I asked her often how could she endure the pain? She prospers all the while having known her for so many years now and she recants 'everybody has their needs' so when legitimate she lends open hearted and open handed. I wish everybody could be like her.

I made a change where it concerned being more aware of the planet. Now I eat holistic foods to bring about a harmony and balance to the earth. I took small steps of change initially reducing my meat consumption to 10% of my daily intake along with taking up yoga six days a week to undo the 40 so long years of abuse to body, soul and psyche. I made a change likewise to use alternative medicine. Small changes to say the least yet change does produce results. Change. Our transformation from unconsciousness to awake to our spiritual endeavor truly accents our being when we awaken to our true nature, to love ourselves first. How is another to benefit otherwise? Modern day spiritual teacher Eckhart Tolle mentions 'all love is self love.' To love one, is assisting everything in creation. To lift up a soul, yours includes adding more depth of meaning. Who benefits from our superficial souls, our personas or its mask of illusion if not only to weary ourselves in an attempt to better on a short term basis?

Love is the answer, then.

I assist in midwifery. I fancy myself a doctor. The midwife that performs in giving birth is given much assistance along with wisdom to pass on to the expectant mother. Too many mothers are over stressed. Rest is emphasized. A true change in this area goes a long way for both mother, child and society at large. We speak to mothers to make small changes if possible in diet, likewise. And we ask the return to a natural pure and holistic cure in nature should mother or baby take ill as oppose to offsetting, taking off balance their immune systems overloaded and overwhelmed as they are at present. It works best to awaken from our stupor. There's too much in the way of pollution which works against anything pure or natural to support and assist us in our growth to conscious behavior.

Yes, we are truly One. And yes, we are the Sun and yes its brilliance in our true conscious enlightened soul. In that state every society of the planet is in love ~ in live, limb in true presence of love within. Everyone on the planet has love within. Who's going to assist the next generation to awaken to our true source within if not we alone as a society in love with our planetary children and call each our own, again? Who to embrace, then?

Our future as a species is just as beautiful and even more beautiful then any sunrise or mountain full of her beauty. Even a spider has her mysterious side to greet with an open armed acceptance rather then a cold stare. Why hate a morning in her beauty ever? Why dismiss our planet's mountains from our view with so many walls and gates and fences ever?

Everyone is in need of play of some form. Everyone is in need of having things taken care of, also. Our balance as humankind is of both spirit (invisible ~ such as love) and physical (material goods) and its needs.

Everyone has a friend at some point in their lives. I wish that were true, though. For the sake of balance, life will have a few lonely folks to accrue to for the sake of being true to Itself. Hope for the sake of being good-natured fate isn't looking in your direction for that one. As transposed in One, the universe abhors a vacuum. For those lonely among us to date as 'Is'~ they say kittens make for good pals. (…whew! Being nice is rough business.) Covered my bases, though.

Everyone is in need of social contact, also. So, why not look more to the spirit part of our needs (our circle of life) as oppose to the linear part of our existence encompassing only of our daily bread, so to speak. Literally and spiritually speaking do it as One so neither is more important than its counter partner.

Choice guys ~ reality rules us not the other way around. Love is our miracle, children our birthright and caring for such everyone gets a turn. Not just the adults or society alone with all the say to the detriment of our souls worldwide. Our planet is in need of our love, also. And when the wind is clean, clear and crisp then much like our friend the cardinal we all take off and land in perfect precision with harmony and grace for everyone concerned.

Love be our grace, forever on infinite as eternal as love would have it be. What was missing was us in love as One. Grace yourself with love and her beauty, then.

Remember a truism ~ everybody has a bad day along with the highest of heights within their soul. Life is relative meaning everything *depends* on another (whether someone or something) to rise or fall within. Ego's included in One so why complain? Even about the weather? *Being the weather* is the answer for we all are true as rain and exist to the glory of love. Not excluding anyone from our infinite love, come please to peace our planet. For only love will essence Itself to One us whole, again.

Butterflies behold our love

Butterflies are flurry midst creation's winged.
Come, let's be its beauty!
Quiet storms are beast loosed
unseen in eyes weary.

Unbutton that shirt nor tie
weary be, yet.
Condors swoop 'neath nested your love as
cacophonous noise your jet.

Silence stillness, unweary me.
Love is *Us* unrhymed
when love is lost, forsakened.
Make not love your crime.

Anna Coffer

Why be with love today?

Some people have all the luck

Senseless to be without our greatest feature, love itself. People are happy most when they have what matters to them most, true? Why is it that many today love being outside on a walking path or on a bicycle even on a picnic as oppose to working themselves slavishly on every turn?

Of course, the answer is easy. To assure yourself you're in balance with your inner needs. Everyone loves being outside, even when the snow is up to their necks! That's because it's playtime. No work today! Too much fun outside, so they close most schools and factories.

Look to nature to assist you in your return to what's essential to humanity. A great windfall is happening to get mankind to be of its divine soul alone. Everyone on the planet is trying to make do with what is transpiring within a day. There's also their more important need, the one thing that matters to every living species on our earth.

Let's look around for a moment. There are so many people that do not have the essentials for their substance. Why is that? Could it be that the illusion of time has taken from the issue at present? Well, yes of course it has. And mightily, too. Let's examine our present mode of conduct once more for emphasis for the next generation to be of benefit of our goodness.

First, children are the most at risk today. The stresses and strains of modern living having rear its head as a means of telling humanity that the very young babies, infants and even those in the pregnant state are being adversely affected.

Everyone is responsible for the next person whether they care for this or not. That's how it works. Why was someone not being told this as it is being here? Why not start today then as though we were planted here yesterday and the right thing is about to take place?

In the goodness of earth's bounty you will be given every delight. This is a wakeup call to humanity. We will all aspire to caring for our own passage. What if the sun were to shine only when convenient? Would that situation occur humanity? No, for most certainly everyone on the planet would suffer, no rather die for the lack of its presence even for a moment would not suffice.

Now let's look at the situation we are facing as a species. Where is the water on the planet to come from? Some say the sky has that one all worked out for us. Absolutely not, that is not the way nature works. She cooperates with everything else.

How nice it is that every person is happy and content to have these essentials. Well, let's take for example what would happen if the sun and the water dis-cooperated with one another like we do with one another on the planet. What would be the sad result? Perhaps the sun would shine so great that the entire planet water system malfunctions or is weakened through non-compliance of its dependent neighbor.

"The sun depends on the water source?" some ask. The sun has needs. We all exist to keep one another on track. When the planetary rotations are aligned in favor of our planet's orbit, everybody gets along swell.

If so much as one particle of our mist is not in favor of evaporating for the sake of keeping ourselves on track, what happens to our planet? Will the water too be weakened for the sake of the pull we have on our moon surface, our sun and Jupiter's orbit, even?

Yes, absolutely! Where are the scientist who will refute the tides of the earth have already been affected by our mismanagement? So too is our planet affecting the pulls we have on our sector. Our moon is off course by not much more than it takes to take the entire universe to jolt at being 'punched' so to speak. Who is managing the universe, then?

Want more proof?

Look at our seas. The largest sea we had on the planet is completely gone. These seas drying out are causing our planet to off-balance, veer off our orbit in need of a 'wheel-balance'.

Nobody wants to die in a 'solar crash' being pulled off orbit due to a weakened watered-down magnetic pull either up or down, sideways or across. Perfect precision on your auto is a must as is with our planetary water system including our rainforest. Where is the power of her, mankind? Null and voided at the hands of our mismanagement, true? Weakened and all for what? So we can manage what matters little. Whatever science has taught will do very little for a conscious enlightened present society which is needed to be planted in love alone, for the sake of everything.

Balance is used to give life. A lack of it will cause accidental injury as in the case of my nephew who at birth was accidently dropped by his attending physician only to the detriment of an entire family. He being bruised caused a neurological malfunction to his body being permanently branded handicapped his entire existence. As a result, mother weakened in her resolve to care for an only child born to it for fear of having another would be mishandled as well. A father who abandoned its mother and child both for fear there would be his conscious to accept the unacceptable as the boy borne was beautiful in every way except to one careless mishap from a otherwise perfect performing doctor who 'slipped' in the management of his care, his patient.

My nephew's inability to function from the neck down is loved and cared for by society. My aunt is loved by those in heavenly places for enduring her pain and shame to have to love, care and be present to his ever-growing needs clear to his adulthood years.

Society, could you please wake up and share? Everything is in common. Love our planet! Save the whales! Most people laugh at those sensitive to our needs as a species. Their humanity is at best looked at with disgust by most.

When we decide for ourselves and the hope is today at best, may we all live in 'Oneness' so that the sun, the universe and even the littlest of those among us ~ mankind and our species survive in the only way that glorifies us as people in management of our future home our planet and that would be in love.

I like talking about our planet with others of likeminded concern so I'll share my e-contact for anyone to speak with on the lines of nature or myself on matters of 'Oneness':

E-contact

Onenessofbeing@annacoffer-onenessofbeing.com

I am gifted to speak with every soul in creation. This is the first of its kind for even stars are privy and open in awareness as my senses accrue to their being present in glory as any rose or peoples of our species. It does help to prove loyal to our planet and our lives as being part of the whole of everything in existence. This humanity is called 'Oneness of Being.'

Much is said and being done in the name of love, bubs. So let's get our soul aligned with the Universe. Love yourself madly! Your soul will thank you for it. 'Oneness' has its privileges!

In the midst of a storm

In the midst of a storm, be quiet
neither be of discomfort. Toward
the Sun follow your heart still.
Storms brew as shadows. Bore

along a yellow caste of floral
life, know we each have another.
Fellows deep within our One
have such episodes of thunder.

Coral reefs of love nor life
have shadows known
to them as loveless such.
Bewilderment, a love is coned

a spiral of depth least we fall.
Bewilderment know no lost nor found.
But wherever, whatever love cost ~
remember it's around.

It fills the heart with glee
so count out its worth.
For whom it does concern
it's worth no less our earth.

Falter none or all
for peace within we be.
Never known but felt
love is a cone, less a bee.

Smiles in a wilderness of lovelessness are we
such our winds of life off key.
Call a tour to life its sum
as love'll have us be.

No sacrifice thru it

Get over the non- activity

Like honey to bees, once in a while a book will come along to not only excite humanity to awaken to its spiritual evolvement but also to assist in helping them to wake up to the only purpose for which they were purported to exist to date, love and its source.

Wake me up when the world is immensely populated so we can have a premise in which to confer our soul to awaken up to before lunchtime, hopefully. Let's talk about love and our situation facing us on our journey toward being One with all that exists. What is missing from humanity today is its most basic need. Any taker's what that might encompass?

True we need food and shelter for such assets make for a peaceful environment to a soul attached to the goodness where welfare of one's person is concerned, true? Yet there is even a more basic need then life itself. What could that be?

"Anything other than life itself would be fruitless," some thought out there is mistakenly transmitting to others on the planet as I speak. Some would say life itself is it. After that, no more good comes from the atmosphere or our planet or from anywhere else because we 'died' and so therefore the issue at hand 'life being worth living' comes into play.

Somewhere down the line when we're dead and gone there are others that replenish our planet and for sure they sense life as being worthy of our every endeavor to encompass it, yes embrace. So, if life in its fullness, full blooming consciousness as/'Is' already happening and always will, then what is the true issue facing our society, person and our will to take care of the essential true need being none other than love itself? Anyone will tell you love is important because it's true. In its very essence is life teaming with all sorts of new activities, and adventures at anyone's disposal.

Love in all its wisdom is here to teach what needs to be learned once and for all for the sake of humanity's pride or lesser of it. Wisdom and its ability is so easy to ascribe to.

Many times man in his folly will decide for itself to do whatever comes to mind be it of wealth, jargon or business otherwise to be that to be important to itself. But is it true that mankind is better off with the lesser none important matter at its disposal?

People the world over have always wanted to be at peace. Most will do anything at this juncture for its prize is of high value to one's mind, body and heart. Even the welfare of the planet is being inundated with lesser more destructive forces to its calamitous situation due to forces either unknown or undisclosed for the best answers to come to the fore.

People of all ages would love to just shake up a few of its majority of humanity and say "Wake up!" People the world over are starving for the one thing that makes sense ~ a spiritual awakening and its by-product, love itself.

Allow me to introduce to you yourself. You may feel you have little or no control in the situation of what is happening on the earth to date. In all honesty, you are the one responsible for every movement that is happening on the planet. Everything contributes to its betterment or destructive nature. This is yin / yang yes /no and up / down or for lack of a better word 'balance.' For the sake of argument this is the premise of all existence known on the human level as 'life'.

Why is it people today love to be fooled rather than see life in a way that contributes to the whole of society, the planetary essential for its function to continue?

Once upon a time, there lived a person all alone. They wanted friendship. All they got in return was very little in the way of true companionship. Love is elusive to many today for many reasons. So let's expound on a few for the sake of getting the issue for once out in the open air so that anyone who figures to argue or wants to discount love as our ally may step up at least and give it a good try as to why they feel the issue should be nullified and forgotten, negated even.

"Children of the Corn" was a movie that helped people to come to the conclusion that the only reason to keep themselves alive for any purpose is to propagate another future of its kind, city dwelling. What of life and its mystery? What in the world would motive a producer of this movie to want more of the same theme, tragic as that one was already referring to living in an existence of a city to bring about a disastrous situation? What of country living? Who would desire to want to live on a planet minus street signs, violence and less of them? Most would, I assure you.

Would a tree planted every hour on the hour suffice society? What justifies a situation of hatred today? Any takers? Is there not enough of that already? Who wants more of a loveless situation? Is the issue of love to be taken lightly even when the entire planet seems hopelessly out of date for its wisdom?

Let's take a puppy for example. Is it not beauty incarnate? Where is the owner of such a beautiful by-product of its wisdom? Listen within, then. Who knows the way of the wind? Where is it going? Where its center? Mankind is in need to ascend to higher consciousness. Its deafening sound due to the lack of it suffices the dullest of sensibilities due to an inability to conform to its source being divine in nature.

I really like as a publisher of peace in the world today to cover as much on this matter of peace as I possibly can. Does the sky look blue today? Of course the entire universe looks like it's one big ball of clay-like substance. In truth, the entire universe is of its divine order, love. Who missed it? We did due to our unconscious, unevolved, unenlightened nature. So, our unloving and untold busy-ness due to mindless thinking with all its clamorous atmosphere permeate us to date. This is not love. Love is felt as 'being' incarnate with its ability to conform to the seasons for just as winter precedes spring, so thus is life's order. For the sake of getting people to love one another finally and without hesitation let's examine the proof of the existence of the planetary alignment to hold out its truth.

Look up at the physical universal. "It's deep," most will say automatically and it is true. For one to be wise enough to make this assumption and it is true of course, let's say for the sake of all involved that the depth of it is phantomless to everyone except those privileged to be of its caliber. Say you understand you and the universe are One and the same being.

How far would up be at that distance to you! The universe is so true to itself that it being of its course in its revolvement is just a little shadowy form at best of it's true nature, the entire gamut of itself. Its truth stands as evidence likened to one being studied by another yet true to its course of study it gets finally the answer of its work ~ in this case knowing you and me and the universe are One indeed without a fallacy to accrue to as never before.

Life is the same way. You are all of it. You are not just an ocean with its depth. You too are the sky and the entire planetary function included. So, what's the big deal around here? Am I just to be here on this planet to serve another? No, helps but you see the conundrum of its forces of Itself being manifested at every moment through existence whereby we exist.

Otherwise, why would anyone want to die, dead some say? In earnest, most would like to stay around the place called earth. It's a nice place when you're happy. I too as an author on peace and its source which is a by-product of nothing other then yourself in cacophonous mode would prefer, no rather hate to be dismissed as a part of the entire whole.

Yet again, there it is. Someone, somewhere, everywhere except to a few conscious evolved enlightened among humanity understand that in order to manifest itself in its entirety would be impossible. And understand, using the naked eye is useless as love being its essence nor spiritless is infinite and formless therefore moot it's absence to humanity ever meaning simply eternal peace 'Is.'

Let's say for example a person wanted to use a telescope to see how space operated. Would the instrument suffice to tell the entire whole of humanity how, when or where our origin began? As such, it would be impossible for form is temporary at best. Eternal love would be dismissed and often is excused at that rate of progress.

For the sake of helping humanity to superimpose for once upon a matter of importance to Itself, let's all do one another the courtesy of being nice first, then ask questions of another as questions too are infinite and absolutely useless as life, space is no-thing and to grow weary in search of another that would be absence and not life giving at all.

Temper questions with a statement, as such would be appropriate now due to an overabundance of formal knowledge. Let a teacher of One suffice.

Due to the nature of stillness, it involves getting away from the mundane to experience life in its fullness regarding our soul as will happen in the near future. Our awakening is of Spirit. Form does not exist in that area for it would dissolve, return to being Itself ~ One with all that is in existence.

Let's take an apple for an example. For expediency to help with the understanding of Itself as all but the core is silly. Let's talk of its 'Oneness'. An apple has a taste. It will not fare to dispose of it until the person who picked it gets its fare share of its goods, true?

Let's say that the apple could talk. What would it say to mankind today so that they could feel what its situation is among such a large field of audience? Would it shiver in embarrassment? Would it cave to the occasion just because it can be heard for once as though a miracle is less on any other occasion? No, it would speak its truth as well as of its alarm for the situation at hand that humanity is facing.

A lack of audience would be its only alarm. Now, due to an extensive audience thus with our excellent yet proficient author as such an occasion as this, you will be privy to hear it speak through 'Consciousness.' (… remember, the wind is you too ~ keep up with the rules this time, guys.) Ants are giggling in earnest retort not to mention all of society as this publication is just another of mankind's attempt to get it to see Itself as love though another's eyes.

Let's suppose for the sake of 'time' the enemy of all that suffices as worth anything meaningful is just that 'time'. 'Time' is the elusive culprit of humanity's crux with existence. Cacophonous of this situation is mostly due to erroneous thinking. Its 'timelessness' that is to be accrued to this time for our existence to be correctly lived. Love is unconditional in its infinite wisdom, true?

Most people like the way humanity is struggling with its ability to gain access with their higher wisdom. Spiritual teachers abound worldwide today yet, which of them produced the apple? So, it suffices to say a higher power being wisdom Itself is producing life as we know it, correct?

Most will refute that this higher personage has any inference with the way humanity is transposing itself on our planet. Wrong. To those who accrue to a higher purpose like saving the whales or saving the planet or mankind from unsavory sources also the looking after and caring for those less fortunate then oneself, its these folks that are not being given notice.

Most will turn a blind eye to their earnest endeavor at best. The unattention being given to these is a shame for their motive is love alone and going without notice lends little ~ no, rather non-support sufficient to encourage their divine endeavor though heavy and burdensome on their soul. Encourage at every turn then not just these who take their concerns to heart, as such is their lot but too for the sake of returning to our 'Oneness' of humanity.

Picture if you will the earth green with more water than plant life. Is it possible to smother one with the other? Is it possible for water to overrule our greenery? Rules matter, truth rules. Same with the animal kingdom, which everyone is a part of ~ excuse the expression that we are part of this class but Oneness dictates what is true not our physical incantation of what truth can understand at a given moment because its bigger than the physical universe, also.

So, doing the math what we get is no-where every time. Now it looks awful but without this premise to rule what is true in reality, we would mess up our entire planet not to mention our water supplies which by the way remain sane despite our disturbed human behavior thrusted upon her soul/being.

Another case at point, our sea life. Why would you want to hear a whale cry for its existence? Is it to hear it in blind ambition, again? 'No,' some at least will say coming out of their sleepful existence of nonconformancy. Following the herd helps when you want to continue on with the entire gamut of the universe in a lost state.

Let's listen to the whale today, then. Who enjoys its sound? Can an ocean wave be missing a friend or foe on its currents of love or loveless existence depending on the one listening? Of course everyone loves the whale but who wants to see that they have safe passage? Most will answer but to what cost to their comfort and convenience? Of course to me, I hear the whale. So does anyone in One mode.

Now, to listen to the whale would bring most to their knees, most would faint. Anyone would want to (hummm…give up the ghost) because they have a true ability to communicate with its higher power which is not only present within the animal but too its listener.

What if the whale were busy to the point of not wanting to communicate with mankind at least not this sector of our existence and so we never get to hear it's beautiful retort of any kind we might be privy to? Then down the road of existence we all go without knowing what or how we affected this beautiful creature who obviously wants to be heard for once and shall, too.

Hear the whale mankind:

"Please humanity, I am not alone in this existence of wanting to be heard. But today is special for all of mankind. I can and do speak. I love my existence as I am sure you love the life you are and very much want to continue on as your species does, too. Love me as you do a child. A beast of the field is also among mankind and is privileged to serve with earnest jest to get people of all sorts to pay attention to its kind, also. Let's all live in a harmony for once, please. Say hello to everything that moves as special as love would have us. Humanity, wake up! You have slept until we all need our love to suffice this once and for all time." "'Love me too, please!" says the crawly creatures of the earth."

Every creature of the planet is an open book to me. They all speak in a harmony of 'Oneness' heard with as a purity of soul to accrue to in our species. Hear baby seals. They are innocent and correct to want us as humans to treat them with the respect and benevolence they deserve as they too are One with all that are in existence.

Formless as love is but closed in ear and heart to those absent to its wisdom there are those today predisposed to its whims to behave in such a way as to allow even our planet to speak. Our planet too has been waiting to be heard, mankind.

Yes, listen with earnest heart to our planet speak today:

"Hello, I am the land you are standing on. I love having my soul exposed for the reason of sensing into the impossible task of healing mankind with what I have at my disposal. There are fruits and vegetables that go unseen by most although I grow them in abundance.

Too many people are inhabiting earth. A billion or so suffices at present. No need to rush to adjust the situation. Just be open to my wisdom for I care and carry each and every one of you to your last breathe within my gates for protection. Love me as you would care for a loved relative. There is no distance in love nor folly. Just do your best. Humans have survived much less then we are offering, so take care to do what is needed of family or foe but do adheed to love first before folly gets its foot rooted deep into the psyche of the material home you call your 'earthly existence.' Follow a simple path, love. In a genuine stance of it, all will suffice of its wisdom. Then joy be your inhabitant ~ as it's eternal."

The earth loves being heard today. I have a special talent of Oneness to hear all creation. That being the premise, allow me to introduce you to our tree species among humanity, too.

Trees are alive with wisdom so with earnest ear listen, please:

"I am a tree within creation. People see me as a 'thing' with no chance to communicate whatsoever. Yet, I am alive. My being is in sore straits. People are in need of waking up to life in a way that makes sense to everything in creation not just for the sake of being in human mode alone with its tree area so unloved. With so little attention to our being, many care little or nothing for us nor our survival. Next time shade is needed for humanity or for our food and yes even beauty for flowers among our branches too are suffering beyond measure, then please follow this simple rule: Love alone will suffice. We need clean water and pure fresh air for these are crucial to our life span. The expediency of our lives are cut short in tragic measures due to an abundance of over activity in the area of lovelessness for our safe existence. Though love is our prime need, please be careful to not walk on the planet too rough, also. Touch us in gentle concern, for our wellbeing is crucial to exist in One mode. Smell our beautiful fragrance or just sit by us. Help comfort our existence, for active attention to our beautiful being would truly be worth its weight in satisfaction to your souls too in a relationship where neither loses ground yet accents our existence together in a cooperative effort for the sake of Oneness to expand despite an atmosphere of indifference in some. Thank you humanity for listening to our urgent message and your willingness to care for a tree. To assist humanity at our fullness to give you our best, we need cooperative effort in this endeavor."

Rock sounds it's thunder

Blessings are of love
comfort another, do
so sounds of soft whispers
enter it ~ pursue

'til honeycombs brighten.
Sing a song so new
its beauty's you...your life.
Beam your light, be you!

A unique way to be
is us on life and light.
Babies coo come wave and bow.
Cones on love shine bright

on evening heavenly canopies
to soften existence, true
and tell their wonder of existence
their beams of bright's but *you*!

Spiritual Awakening

*Consequential love besets us back to the
old order ~ a nuisance at best*

To date everywhere we go we manage to hear a sound that sounds something like "move over and allow the universe to be in a state of being that makes sense to the soul or higher awareness." At present everyone wants to be included in the one area that helps to get the message out for humanity to better itself.

There are many ways for that to happen. First, such a message has been carried by teachers of higher consciousness, this book included. As we as a species move closer to awakening in spirit, everything will align with the Universe as '*Is*'.

In total darkness everything is alive and seen on a level of spirit. This comes only once in never. This is my awareness, though. Some will equate no light with a negative connotation. This is a fallacy at best. Let's revert for reminisce sake to the old adage "Live and let live." Many times people will go with the familiar or what is comfortable as society in their learnt mode of conditioning. For many this way of being suits the mind in a satisfying way for them. In our to date male oriented society this does not suit every aspect of our being like love would aspire us as a species, though.

Consequently waking up spiritually as a species, we humans are just about there. How much more pain and suffering would it take to get to the crux. A solution is warranted. Thus, this book and many congrats to the souls who have found their way to it. Plus, we as individuals will be waking up in a peaceful more endurable environment that compliments the divine.

Being sacred in our 'being' allows us to be infinitely kind meaning also we are capable of being good too in unlimited supply as love is of this measure or should I say measureless proportion. Love has its way and we need do nothing but accept it as being here today for us to utilize its special curing on our souls likewise our societies across the world. Was love ever absent? Many will say yes, otherwise no need for such a book as this or even the bible for humanity at that level would be conscious and awake spiritually. The literal sun does not shine as in the spirit realm, they are in no need of it. There is a differential in our way of being. For humans the sun is present as a form to function for light.

Because to some, love is all but missing from our issue of what truly matters. It's here we have come to accept that now is as good a time as any to propose it upon our mental, physical and emotion 'awareness'. Love is perfect in every aspect. It looks for the best and wants to be helpful. Love has a way of being first to some but to many today it's in short supply. Why the contradiction, then? Let's take a look at what a loveless society would do to hurt, or otherwise harm those that look for the togetherness of "Oneness" and the harmony it could produce as a helpful hand to another.

Let's say a person is in need of a friend. How many people can honestly say they have that one special person that allows them to be themselves and care for them, also?

As love would have it, it's a give and take situation. At best some are givers and so...*wella!* The secret to the universe on what it takes to have and keep a healthy relationship afloat is nowhere near as a secret as some would have it. Being truthful is a simple recipe to keep a healthy relationship along with a symbolic banner that reads "Look, I'm flexible." Without the ability to give and take ~ bow to the needs of the many or another as such, where would that leave us either in a relationship or as a society, even? Not much mystery to the failure and misgivings of what was amiss, then.

What of a romantic situation with another, too? Where is the 'flexibility' when needed? Are there children involved or grandparents or even siblings to be taken into account? Let's take a look at this situation closely. Whenever you have a situation where there are two people in love, they are in need of 'space'. What is that, space?

Space is a special place inculcated into the species that allows another to be themselves without interference from another so that what needs to transpire for itself in a healthy circumstance can. Accordingly, there are other needs to be taken into consideration. Let's look at the family as an example here. What if a baby cries? Who is the best suited to answer the babies' needs? It is its Mother, true?

But look at our society. Many will agree also that the child is best with a father only with no mother to impose nurturing. The gift of reproduction can come only through a woman therefore much folly accompanies her baby absent of her love to partake of.

Part of our waking up to the sacred divine arrangement of love for the family, would it be best to sit around and wait for the cry of our young in society to be ignored with no answer? Is our young and their cry for attention being satisfied? In what way? Is humanity clothed worldwide? Do they have what is sufficient as far as housing or a healthy meal even? "Big undertaking," some would say! And it is true, likewise. Impossible? Yes and no at this juncture of our evolving species. Love is the key to all management on our planet, then.

What of our domestic wildlife, even? Would even a lowly cow do best to be in alignment with the universe ~ a harmony that is being taught as living is a conscious way for us? As a cow, most are left just to wander in a field as oppose to letting nature have her way with it. In the wild, a cow acts differently knowing instinctively even how to birth her own calf. Does that make her a genius or is nature knowingly doing its job to see to a need for her calf's delivery?

Nowhere is there a map to say, "Hey, get off the planet and start a society on Mars, won't you." But in a sense that is an ideal to some who are unconscious to the needs that are imposing themselves in our care. Look at our water supply and too creation as well as our forestry. These are under our care. Do we as a species neglect the obvious for the sake of convenience? Not good management.

Why is the world in such a state as it is today? First let's examine the issue of what makes it tick. Anyone can write on the subject of consciousness, obviously. But in what way is humanity being affected by the people who are concerned for the planet to date? Who cares for our creation? We do, it is under our supervision.

Happily the entire gamut of the universe is of Oneness. Suppose the universe were to be replaced with an uncoothed, unloving species? What then? Would not the inhabitations of our planet be in an upset state of affairs? True, for it is to date and that's the issue on the table. Thus, in this book written on the awareness of humanity much is amiss among mankind when it comes to loving itself, true?

Love people as One, then. The return to One is simple, effortless even. Do you like something? Good for you. Be about it in earnest because nothing less will produce the desirous result to your mental, emotion and spiritual welfare as a whole being. That is what transpires.

Cutting people off at the knees that are happy is wrong. Play nice together. Boys...hummm. They have mothers most of them so their issue is covered not to mention societies and their wisdom to correct a misguided youth is available as conformity is relative yet effective meaning beach clothes at the shore works fine but in a classroom of education import, beachwear is a nonsufficient attire.

So too our current society, its functioning sufficient enough yet in our 'waking up spirituality' to the reality of our ways these too will come under revamping as justice is akin to peace as well as aligning ourselves with our divine nature.

Waking up to our true nature is upon us. Love would have us be what? Like, *kind* people for one. Takes the guesswork out of what made us miserable. If you see somebody nice, be like that. Don't oppose their truth any longer. They could use any assistance from any sector of our world, society or even the soul as it would be construed as being 'cared about' and feeling loved and supported to its truest self.

A day is 24 hours, yes and no. Love is infinite, timing is everything. Love as you would have your most prized, cherished possession dealt with in the hands of another. That is how it works with the heart. Giving of what matters most carries a great and endearing price worthy of sharing with another. Doing so, compassion has its glory in our entire planet. Such a future in One is upon us. Have it your way. Sweet is a day to a kitten and a waterfall and a gorgeous skyline at dusk, so please come join the enlightened among creation. We welcome your fearless attire to be One with love as us in peace.

"We could have made it out of the woods long time ago!" cry those in need of their spirits to awaken to this blessed moment, the only place love abides by the way. Truth loves wisdom. Which came first, though? A continuation on this will be in our next series – You Can't Take Your Credit Card With You When You Go book 3 as a three part series in a trilogy of "Who runs this place when love is us, again?" is one of the themes addressed so humanity has safe passage without questioning anything. For in an absolute resolve, there growth continues her ascension to *Be of One*.

There is a question and answer section to oppose conventional wisdom. Being of divine source is crucial yet satisfactory when warranted by our call to release us from pain at any cost. It's a mode. We're there. Students of One are never found, they're waiting to start like yesterday. Pain and suffering excuses the obvious alignment shift some have named metaphysically in laymen's terms, 'being selfish and got away with it, too!' (…in simple English this time.) Growth, in the direction of maturity and lending credence to people of understanding of the deep, no rather the deepest of wisdom ever to inhabit humanity on a once in a lifetime miraculous event of coming to grips that our soul is full of wisdom (*sigh*) but we didn't use it guys. Waking up to our divine soul delivers us from our pain, suffering and anguish imposed through our conditioned, limited, unconscious situation to date. Not me and you, more like me or you due to our backward mode of existence. In truth we are One. Being for being, I like me sweet.

The old order was amiss with us separate, ego ruled. The solidarity of Oneness bonds us to be helpful, courteous and polite. It's a quieter mode, as such is the way of spirit while it accrues to being 'still' within although outer storms of existence on the surface of humanity are perceived undisturbed from those who journey into consciousness by way of wisdoming itself to behave in a clear manner to accept growth for the betterment of the whole of humanity. *We are One.*

In a three part series of "Where is my life before love can get it?" holds true as men are also awakening. Its Mystery is not absolute. Men have a fear of commitment. This produces males who know of love's due and will even cough up or as they have jargoned its cute mathless equation by retorting, "Choose your battles carefully before you approach a woman." Delicate in nature, these sweet ladies are in their no-thing attire, huh guys?

Happenstance ~ look it up, truly relevant here. Not to love has its absolute, also. Obviously then, being absolute in its relevance holds true and encompasses humanity ~ for fear too exist among us. Yet, in its sphere of caring as well as its counterpart, indifference looks to love Itself once more. See me in book 3 then and be of its grace ~ love that is.

Whisperless

I love you more.

Silence is as silence is being. How silent are you? Loud noises have their approval in a moment of rejoicing as in heaven so on earth.

Why is society in gloom so much of its existence? Seventy years or so is not that long. Joy is infinite, remember? Can we joy our planet? It's not a thing, it's no-thing. Its joy is barren because it depends on our being at peace. Why should rules like these apply to anyone least the earth our planet?

Is joy the culprit? A joyless soul lives alone somewhere. Could company be the answer? A slight smile or grin? These are whisperless gestures of love and concern for another.

Magicians poof their joy into existence. That's why people clamor to see their performances. They live their lives on the edge. They excite the young in their wonderment to know how things appear and disappear at the will of the magician. Lowly society of mankind, why bow the head in despair? Some may chagrin "I hate my life!" What words would cover your true state though, to be of One with life? Then look at a kitten and peace your soul. Comfort yourself. Many have small pets, a puppy or a tank of fish to while away moments of peace with.

More work will take away from this space. Where the space for us? Can we make room, give space to another to be? In a mode of peace alone we cherish everyone. An unlikeable situation for a war monger or two.

And yes, oh weary over-worked, overwhelmed us as we watch another ~ could love unweary us as a whole here, likewise? An enclave of desire to bring back life in its fullness. To unweary a soul, to lighten its burden is peace itself. Going within demands change from (gulp) status quo. (...oh please do not hurt my children)

Should we call names should one hit a cord so true even birds sing along "Hey, waking up cost." At what cost will we wake up to peace? War is the answer for some. Peace, likewise. For myself, I am One with all there is in existence.

Love be us whole. I am too hard in my soul to cry and yet it amazes me I do. I sense lost of society's good so great to return to us once more that it's my only desire. What is good?

Sounds much like asking "What is truth?" Oh no. Point but don't blame another. We just went over that one a moment or two ago which is the illusion. We are without time. Oh humanity, please wake up!

What is good? It is who we are. Our essence when we identify with it identifies us as sovereign ruler over creation with pure motive. We are the keepers of our societies. Being good requires much our soul today to harmonize with divine source as above so below. (...I said that with a straight face. Oh! And I own a kitten. I plead don't harm my kitty!) I wish no harm nor malice nor name calling to offend the nice in another.

Could we please just all get along? (...I have the biggest grin)

Love can break a bone.

Love is consequential to our moment of peace. Love can silence war.

Love (have mercy) ...don't break my back here, humanity.

"I didn't do it, I ate the cake" is an oxymoron. Did anyone on the planet go anywhere? Oh, we still have this *'be nice to another issue'* still rearing its peaceful endeavor to get us to love (gulp...no GULP!).

How am I to continue in this loveless state, humanity? Do we love less a bluebird? Some say they fly around to give happiness? Has one landed on anybody's shoulder lately? The evening news broadcasts vividly we are unconscious, still.

Okay, I cease and desist where we need to improve to become One. Only buy the next book if you have to, humanity. I wrote three books about our return to consciousness, a trilogy. They took two days, actually 2 ½ to get written. And heaven (...and I use the word lightly, humanity) can suffice a differential of truce be it of life, limb (gulp) or our pursuit of (...be still my fear within) happiness.

Justice has a way of being. Beginnings are endings. So suffices a fool to negate our true essence to be nice to each other. What future without our participation meaning change? (...this computer hasn't exploded yet so I'm going to hang in there) I hope (...there is a silence in creation so wide and so deep the universe is tiny in comparison) we change to better our future. Love please anything, humanity. (smiling)

"I hate positive people!" some recant.

I bless people without hope, though.

"I hate love returning!" cry big babies who were losers to begin with for being mean-spirited, selfish nor self-center enough to realize they were unconscious. Unconsciousness means jestly 'forgive me for being a jerk.' What person wants to cause pain to another, on purpose even? Even still, love knows no bounds. It will assist even your butt.

"I want my Mommy to know better to rear me right!" cry those still holding others responsible for their actions.

There is a clause that mandates you cannot always be in charge. Just the same, most Mothers worldwide gave the figurative penny 'their last coin' to no avail. So why blame Mommy or women to boot. We have a society bearing grudges on these poor innocent victims of our *just not wanting to support or adjust a schedule or two* out of 'Hey, this is highly inconvenient for me at this moment to babysit' (here or there).

Babies need love, too. (I loved writing this book)

I'll calm a nerve or two out there by mentioning 'the Lord repays.'

Can we support anyone in legitimate need in society, then? Miss Penny is a saint. You are a saint too if giving without anything less than a pure motive. More of such people make for a happy planet. Yes, consciousness is certainly going to make headway with some selfish area out there today.

Mercy seat is open today. Any takers? We live lives of quiet despair. Some are loud though and unwarranted. Take time to peace the planet. (…what do you want?) I'm a girl. I want peace on earth. That's my answer.

Peace be us within, please.

We are all One

*Let's say we allow this to be ~ who
has love to share with whom?*

I am in love with life again. And just in time, too. My three daughters
have grown and the last has just left the house. My heart would love
to just be with each and every one of them. They feel otherwise, I'm
sure.

I wrote a few sonnets in the perhaps we all do want to be loving the
world over I'd have something I'd like to share of our goodness. In
wisdom love is beautified. I love my life on wholeness anyway I can be
from love. The metaphor 'Kite' whenever used in sonnet will represent
our One, to be whole in our heart again for true wisdom returns as **Us**
being for our good to win over our less then what's worthy our starting
over amidst adverse 'no' (…we didn't eat the cake) or our 'naught.' To
be inconsistent with our good is so not workable, true? So, please read
on. Blessed be and sure hope you like my little verses:

I climbed on the back of a turtle

I climbed on the
back of a sea turtle,
and flew to the moon
and drew to me

waves and oceans and
currents and tides.
Now the
moon is me.

I brought back home moonbeams inside,
it's true.
NOW and moon and me are glue

'cause rip tides of love gone wrong turned around
are useless, but moonbeams
are fun

when tides and rhymes and cockleshell bells ring,
beyond the senses
in One.

Who reads and writes
both in wind and rain,
come hither
Sun of One.

You can't see the wind
or right a weather vane,
but weather is true
as rain

'cause castles made out of
air and sound,
are not the usual
bane.

See me in the wind
hear me in a roar,
can't distinguish a bear or cat
then you, I'd rather ignore.

It's hard for city folk
to know when nature's around.
They run right past her
both feet on her ground!

Slow down! Be the rose for once.
You haven't got a clue!
Why the clouds beam bright their soul
but you did not know you.

A cloud you are in majestic One.
I love this part so true!
'Cause even a mighty timber tree
can cause the wind to do

service to it day or night
love with every breath,
ever missing from the One
is timeless life, in depth.

Best friends

I have a friend
dear to me,
she likes what I like
so it's easy to see

why we get along so well
and comfort the other,
and laugh out loud
and buffer life's thunder.

Noise is loud
she speaks in peace,
I save the last kindness
for you, Denise.

No thanks in pride, the strong or the proud
you're sweet and work hard to the bone.
Call me in moments of tired weariness
I'll never leave you alone.

Suffer not, I'll bear your load
you suffer in silence enough,
to kill two bears at the height of their battle.
Struggle not, for you're tough.

Your courage is a lion
you plant both feet on the land like a kite,
since the lord in you will never give in
to a man that's wrong in his might.

His money can buy and sell souls
but you and me like to live free,
to give of the heart when given the chance
'cause love's like bees on a breeze.

Girlfriends are special.
I need you, Denise,
'cause life gets pretty lonely 'round here.
You come from the east

you come from the Sun,
everything's in common cause we're One.
Love the day as special as you can
'cause the day will come

when life is done and
through down here,
and you home return
to the sky and the air.

Comfort your children
show them what's right,

give them your guidance
guide them in god's Light.

You have a heart that
brings me to my knees,
can't find another you
you're unique, Denise

who needs me, still
and wants a friend,
to bough and wave
come hither again.

Denise knows the kite
I know Daddy,
I help her out
I carry her caddy

to golf in delight
not over a ridge,
but in a cavern
between a bridge

of wonder and light
merciful kin,
to befriend the loss
to lose to win.

'Cause nature's best is not for sale.
I ran and gave a squeeze,
to justice, love and god's great Light
disguised as you, Denise.

bunny, the Lord and innocent I

I bought a book
and couldn't wait
to look inside and read it.

It came with tears
and bloodstained years
of glory, girth and sonnet.

Who took the rainbow
and made it straight?
Not the lord or I.

We see it circled
curved and bowed,
adorned between the sky.

I saw a rabbit hop before
but not like this, you see
the rabbit made a funny sound
then hopped right up to me.

I said, "Hello" and the
rabbit nearly died.
He knew he stood before a majestic One,
the Lord and me inside.

The rabbit spoke, but not in bunny
he spoke of cruel existence,
since now he could declare before the Lord
exsequential innocence.

"A bunny is not decadent,"
the bunny said to the lord and me.
We sat down to listen to his innocence,
yonder 'neath ye' ole girth tree.

So the bunny hopped before us
now that makes three
the bunny, Lord and innocent I
beneath that ole' girth tree.

The bunny spoke in rhythm and rhyme
and told of tales so true,
it made the Lord and I shiver.
We never had a clue!

How did the bunny get his resolve
to tell the news so clear,
since the Lord, not I could hear
a teardrop through the air?

A raindrop cries, not stomp its feet
like bunny and me when mad,
a raindrop falls and soars above
in air of loud not sad.

So the bunny hopped away
vowed never to return,
to a place of girth to listen
since its hop was fully earned.

Its qualities does teach
to mankind, "Do not fear,
for the lord is great and kind
and can create a big, long bunny ear!"

Like bunny there
hopping at noon,
to walk is impossible
since his hoppers are in tune

with nature
and wisdom on his side.
The moons adores his
laughing pride.

He knew the bunny spoke then listened,
who wants to whine and kick and plea?

The lord stands beside a bunny...
besides you and me.

I once heard a turtle talk
of truth and lovelorn loss,
I wonder why the lord provides
for such a little cost

'cause the turtle was sad and blue
and needed rest from man,
to stop the turtle now would bring
his shell to high demand.

"I need to talk to the bunny,"
said the turtle with a glee.
"He knows my plight but nowhere in sight,
I need his girth and plea."

"Stop man from being bad to us!"
shouted the turtle in high voice hymn.
"I need my shell to protect me from harm,
I need it like a friend!"

So the Lord and I walked up to the turtle
and said, "How art thee?"
The turtle regressed in the shell,
since he thought it only me.

The turtle shivered, rattled and rolled
kicked and screamed and yelled,
"I need my shell no more since you arrived,
since from heaven you fell!"

"I have two Suns" said the Lord.
Bunny and I were amused, since the earth
has one and I own none
the thought was bemused.

"Take my hand," said the bunny
to the turtle. "Walk with me.
I know a place to sit,
yonder 'neath ye'ole' girth tree."

So they hopped and walked together
since friend not foe they are.
"We are One," they said,
"never be a Scare

or wound or hurt or bite or
scratch. Just be nice to me."
I learned a lot that day,
yonder 'neath the ole' girth tree.

The tree said, "Look,
I listen to the lord all the time.
I do my best to bend and shade
or breeze in god's good time.

I'm a One and speak like The One.
Listen, hear the wisdom of the tree.
Love the air don't pollute it.
Breathe life free!"

I see the dove and the
dove sees me,
we fly together in the sky
because I am the breeze.

The lord is here, too
the space in between,
where raindrops fall
and I learn to beam

bright light from One
not two or three,

'cause the wind's got a friend
in you and me.

I saw a tree say,
"I am the Lord.
I give mercy
shade and more.

I feed them fruit
the lord in me,
but they don't recognize
me in a tree."

The Sun is me, too.
I like to shine!
The lord is us,
One of a kind."

Turtle, rabbit, cloud and me
we looked upon the lord in glee,
happy too we were to sing
in heaven's tone let out on wing.

As a jewel sees me

Why be blue in a yellow state
hence red and green are true,
deny not this whence it's borne of
mystic love once blue.

I cry at times 'cause life's my pain
of strife and loveless blue,
have mercy love from above
please, hate pain as I do.

So low my up is drenched
in tears. This mellow state,

beckon me once more my within
since kindness too's its estate.

Causal of delight and sing
beckon me above.
I love, I love, I love so true!
Wisdom's as above.

Fire flight due of its wing
save me from this loveless gust,
as mellow blue never knew
such pain 'neath bereft's disgust.

Peer now, oh yellow state!
See mellow pink in new,
a gasp of love's breath within
above this state of blue.

Yellow
and blue
are still me
true.

Cascades of floating meadows
bring spiritual waterfalls.
I am as both are me, now
so dusk to dawn calls,

"Wait, I'm slow!
You're moving in a round!"
causal of delight doest sing,
as coral blue reef's waves pound

on shores up above.
My head's of mystic blue,
I soar above among boundless winds.
See casual's life's bright jewel.

As a jewel sees me
we beckon bright her brilliant light
of blue and yellow, too.
Flights amidst core bright light.

Sing, sing, sing
of love and joy so true!
Thank you for this plate of life
both yellow and misty blue.

Win sometimes when it comes to love

From January – June on a cold dark night
Alaska has a dark side to remember,
May – September is somewhat nice
but blurry again in December.

Still in tune with the moon

"No circus to perform for,"
said the moonbeam, still.
"No one to talk to except
this fish with one gill.

Useless to some
but mighty still,
is one with two legs
but never one gill.

A fish is my friend
I like our company,
I never remind it
I need a soft key

a tune of reminder
is one on a gill,
to talk of a savior
from morning 'til

the day of delivery
I stayed up late,
to watch a miracle
never debate

if One is alive
or dead until,
you walk in my shoes
and give me your gill.

If I need to breathe
help me please,
I like my life
I like the trees.

Help earth recover
give it a gill,
give it a breath
so we can be,
still.

A miracle to behold
not half or 'two'.
One is enough
to pull us through."

Breath above on wing

Where is this life
where dusk to dawn calls?
It's wisdom is in beauty
as man falls from its cause.

If beauty is us
where then the wind blows?
On gusty winds of breaths soar
known only in the soul.

I saw a duck once
or twice told true,
wing spans above earth
as love does, too.

Flight of a bee
me, yet you
soulful soar of breezeful gust
its hour is our due.

Love is a word
but true, a must
of mystic winds
for it blows as you and I in dust.

Winged on winds
of breath above,
doest sing when angels wing
come love disguised in doves

on mystic planes of mist.
Flight soar core me
follow a must,
to grounds midst cavernlorn seas.

Have heaven sung to you lately?
It sings to me on key,
in infinite colors on yellow yet you
intertwined, see?

Run with me in blue skies above
our head. Love lives in lore,
as wisdom's but a tone in us.
Who reason love's got more

for us then hate?
We knew love was bold

now face a plate of love above,
love's not new, it's old.

Missed it, huh?
Mystic me to tell all,
of love and beauty gone a rye
and man's boundless fall

from grace and love
and beauty, too.
Have it back this moment,
stay true to love and you.

Stories are told
and given a feather,
for love is us
come any weather.

*

I write a simple sonnet
some say rough and not,
give it plenty love within
words come to the tot.

Magic has a simple sound
rough edges are not glee,
see a line move from its center
notice you and me.

Together the line
moves 'round the Sun,
got plenty of time
to One.

Flower

Smell not my beauty
see me for my worth, though.
Tigers listen in heightened sound
as I know such a sound, its bow.

Currents wave and bounce and beam
full force to tell of late,
I cried once in a garden of Getseth
full bloom adorned, a gate.

No one sees my heart, though low
saddened by this place,
no one sees my aches nor pain
midst heavenly conscious space.

Comfort now this lovelorn soul
of 'One' place, anew.
Whence a garden of Eden within as such,
graceful doe her due.

An ocean weathers us

Ocean or sea mesmerizes
a soul on One.
Go within, free up its good.
See a soul or none

will see it as humanity.
Cry as a baby does.
If love borne arrived on neigh.
blessed is a soul because

it feels like love, come hither.
Love us all on its thunder.
Cry or not, it will.
Half our whole, we're under

yet see a wave crash the shore.
"Who felt its mighty roar?"
asks us, beckoning bright our soul on love.
To eternity our love's no chore.

Breezes of myriad of waves
beckon us to be,
of life's good and wonder
have us as we be

for naught nor might will change
this mighty hand above,
called love's good from heaven
as doves call us their love.

Beam now a light of consciousness
so bright on ocean seas,
that sail midst wonders…
wait! Come breeze

with me on this!
For only life is true,
give your hand to another.
What's a fool to do?

Love
is true,
love is me.
Love is you.

Bee – A bumble of love

Love has a name
us and we.
Love me
as a bee.

Fly upward toward to the light
land softly in its midst,
of breathless Oneness.
Wonderment's its kiss.

You are blessed
from afar,
in divine love
whence you are.

So come! Forward for us humanity.
Love's in a whisper, not a shadow or cry.
Love's in a bee
come fly!

"You're the one we talked of!"
says heaven from above.
For love called you within its gates,
you're known as its dove.

Honeycombs aren't sweet
they wither midst heavens gates.
Carron feathers have known their pride
nor can't sustain us. Wait...

sweet is our lives'
on justice's return.
Sweet , our hearts arrived.
Love is us learned

that true love waits
when prides on high.
Lowly us
not pride.

Stand before a
mighty wall,

melt its center
least we fall.

Heaven catches a mighty man
least he fall from grace,
whispers softy within
known as human race.

Love is whole ~ One

Islands love her waves, assured.
Shells adorn her body.
Life's abreeze come June nor September
whence love's ignored. A dove key

borne of love as all know
its merrier come June,
lessons learned in love means learning
June is One on noon.

Bright's her star in the sky,
Cirrus her melody.
Melancholy a moment in two,
An atom split softly

for anyone, anywhere anytime
to see love in action.
How's it for love to come calling?
Like weight lifted knowin'

we caused a rift, glory caused.
Put out our light, our love.
For love of anything is due now.
Bewinged midst love's return, its dove.

One

Good morning sunshine
love's in light,
of today's wonderment
work nor right.

Breathless kiss
of wonderment's anew
twice shy, once bitten.
Thought you knew.

For love just 'Is'
when love's on key.
So loosen that tie,
follow me

to love on key.
For mercy's it
when love is right.
Come! Let's sit.

Love will die in you ~
our love's off key, see.
Re-live us right.
Love's our beauty.

Love is here to discuss us whole,
better now than never.
One of us is all we have
come highlander nor wither

to move a mighty fortress of hate.
Love alone can do this, never stall.
Hatred falls as scales
from eyes who hear love's call.

Peace's Assurance

Variable to truth known in the soul
a cost of love, true.
Peace cost ~ as love bears you whole
lend your soul to another, they're you.

Peace ~ a beam of light. Conscious
being, thought ignored.
But fruitful being of jewel's light
cacophonous deemed nor chored.

Heavy is to burden
as brilliance is bright light,
love has a way of being
bend for another. Give like

tomorrow never ends.
So there we have the key.
Us on life as *Infinite* us, given
bright be.

Gleamed in Matrix

Sat by a sea to write in patience
but the sea rhymed me,
it caught me off guard
to write like the sea.

My soul's gleamed in matrix
I write in air too,
now life is a beach
got nothing to do.

Being is first, last and true.
being has worth beyond a fool.
There's much in a
unhurried rest. Relax, here's your clue!

Soul on bright

Playful gusty winds never known
for we over do.
Calm down, slow our pace.
Who knew?

Hurry, hurry, hurry!
Hate a hurried pace,
justice's in a slow call
to calm the human race.

A playful smile's
a turtle on a crawl.
Children yelp and holler,
"Love's come to us all!"

Better late than never
just know love's around,
lost your place in a hurried pace.
'Be' the crawl, The Power's in Now

there's little time to play.
Children know life's Mystery,
they play come
rainy day.

'Hold a candle be the flame'
backward, forward truth.
The beauty is in simple things
like sunsets, rises and you.

As One has a way of being
be about a day,
alive and wise and beauty
is us on no delay.

Waiting is an illusion as peace is infinite, still.
Quiet a mind once confused,
wisdom's got more for us ~
come! Life beams us amused.

Bees fly in June

Little bits of flurry wings
fly to get around,
when the air is warm and
June comes around.

Little bits of flurry balls
of life do seem,
little when compared to us
but life has its being

of love and truth
and good from above,
and love has us
new in its glove

worn to fit
least we falter,
to hold true our lives
in wonder.

Mystic life where rainbows
glow and shine their bright.
Mystic life of myriads of miracles
daily show their light

in love come June
or we be not
for love – right or wrong
it's got

loads of sweet honey
to grasp our merry flight rear,
in mystic wear of love and light.
Where angels thread not dare.

*

Core soarer
on a bat tour,
money needs no need.
If I could only
fly away to find,
a penniless man in need.

*

I like to breeze
in a tour of
core sonnet of myrrh.
Be with the girl
in a bat cave of sonnet.
Just a stone is a pearl.

Angel

Comets don't land
they fizzle out in space,
peered among mankind to find
Now as new, well graced.

Whence angels sing
"Be us in One!"
As canes sweet and striped of life
cake known as you, have fun!

Sweetened in love, act just like us
hollow barriers stop not us or another
beaming mystic ~ core insight
toned by love its cover.

Season's change and so do I.
Butterflies fly windsongs to sing,
"Give me your hand in honest retort."
It's love let out on wing.

Life on Now

What is this to me
on a night of just being free?
Suppose life disappeared from view
causal of doubt in pain, see?

Where the soul to discuss its whereabouts'?
So, doubt not nor ruffle of feathered cuff be.
Butterflies change as life rearranged,
then give love her due in infinity.

*

Concrete word wise to some
are hard on the ear,
I like my life done in nice
not in hum-drum gear.

Does the moon sing?
Yes and no. Let's see,
I have a note to deliver
in love tone melody.

Will the moon be mad
not to sing and be heard,
by angels and moonbeams galore?

Has the lord been in danger
from rough seas and breeze,
without One above to adore?

*

Dark side
nobody but the cold,
'cause who can shine what's from behind
and never tell its told.

I talk backwards
forward is right for some,
but what is forward could be backward
then who's the One to run?

I can't flee
I'm busy being me,
not you or another

so don't fight the feeling
next time I talk of Oneness,
sense the light and thunder!

*

Even a 'no' is a 'yes' in One
curdled beyond time.
A rose her velvet flows
who wrote the rhyme?

*

Why be weary in aurora
bend a cloud to breeze,
how can a sonnet cloud my thoughts
and bring my mind to its knees?

Dawn matrix

Not long ago
or never 'til the morning be at One,
cut short the hand of mellow drama
come forth hither Sun.

Breathless One of love and fury
on breezeless moonless night,
because the night has sorrow blues
be of its brightest lights.

Of the soul because it's One
in love and beauty, still
love a kite of wonder dust.
Bee balm honey's till.

Be free to sneeze away
climb a tree instead.
Go outside be free,
be my daily bread.

To give of self
is better than money,
to give of the heart
to kite with a honey.

Freeze tone kind mind wanderer
see her flipless thunder,
I know of none that light the Sun
like moon dust, water and thunder.

Morning is me
I light the way,
within wisdom
delight in decay.

Dawn is two
not three or six,
I wrote the sound
semantics not…it's matrix.

*

Wise in the mind
to give away ring,
certain to cope
never to cling

to others but help
stay on the ground,
bee in my honey.
Who wrote the sound?

*

Breathe a sonnet clear ~ be about a bear.
A bear can whisper a sonnet about a bear,
but can a bear
breastfeed the air?

*

With illustrious locks of time beyond,
go slow.
A hurried hand knows no lost,
inside cold winds blow, though.

Knots in the hands of time
curdled twisty me, bend to get ahead.
If I fell on my face, the human race
could be me lost instead.

*

Little did we know
life blew in two,
one is yellow and pink
the other gray and blue.

'Yes' and 'no' a mighty tyke
of 'yes" I am today,
tomorrow may be sad and blue
acceptance of the way.

*

I tell of you and me made of
love and beauty beyond moon's glow,
since love has its head in clouds made by moon's dust
and sing in cognate soul.

I have a love for the night so starry and bright
made from Life's own hands.
Love it or live in its universe
on second-hand guesses from man.

Don't talk to me from a stance of 'yes'
my life does that with me just fine,
talk to me from doubt, I'm a seer
now moonbeams can rhyme my rhyme.

Guessing gale, guess again
love is a blowin' a tune,
of love gone right least mistletoe's night
of wonder is sung come June

of a journey so great I live out my dream
life's here so untold,
with mercy and bright winds of change at the helm
'cause Light has its own kind of glow.

*

Why wander about
on earth of dust and more,
give a clue a blast of you
know amore as a cure.

130 – *Anna Coffer*

I ran down a road
and saw a dust bowl
didn't want to turn around,

I fell on my face
to know my own grace,
as honey cute as sound.

Ancient mind wanderer
knew no grace,
gave money without clue

to grace the place
in love not might,
I give up space for you.

So don't cry or be sorry for doing what makes sense.
Lord knows the day will come,
when mind makes up its torrid affair
let reign of One be done.

No mercy without love
no love without the key,
I have the right to know my job
as being mercy,
be.

Love of self is alright
when everything's okay,
but when the needy need a hand
it's best to save the day!

*

It flows against with me inside
I get a little ride,
on swirls and worlds and winds and tides
of symbols made of pi, π.

*

Of infinity deep
to touch the sky,
be in my breeze
angels can fly.

Depth Sun
going deep,
knew the Sun
would cry.
To know itself
as One of us,
a lair of wonder
pride.

*

Everybody's got to have a hobby
gotta' have some fun,
mine's a bow and arrow
yours is a gun.

Don't hurt me, I'm pink
blue is your color,
sadness has a way of being
harm not a brother.

*

Blue note
red note,
white note
you

same me
same you,

same One.
Who knew?

*

He left the light on this time
I wanted him to be,
closer than a brother
more like me.

I like pink and lace
and clouds in mystic grace,
I like mystic mysteries
he wants sad embraced.

Nothing wrong with the other
everyone has space,
know me as different you
and play with form in grace.

*

A causal of One run to the Sun
be me for a minute.
I gave it my all I took so little from all,
take a look at the senate.

Why cry at night in the soul
when the wind agrees to take a moment to be?
Why not savor the moment and cry later
to be a moment for tea?

*

What is the soul? A person or a whatever,
something or someone.
Everything in existence is me and you and breath,
so away from the Sun are some.

*

Bring back desire for love and fire
love the soul it's Me,
though many are lost and found in One,
loving it all is the key.

*

Say it and it's backwards do it and reframe together
be it and sing a happy tune,
why wait for forever to begin when the wind swims in love
of morning, yesterday and noon?

*

Who's inside of me upside down, sideways and
not at all?
The Almighty as ice and cold and breeze.
Dutiful soul I saw.

It softened in a blow of six
I'm a tree, too
gave away my milk and honey
now I yearn for you.

Not the way of the One
give to not in need,
useless to court two of us
One's of magma sea.

Seer of the soul
soft in One. 'Two' is for the bee,
sweet in sound, soft and round
honeycomb cognate tree

of everlasting life
us and you and we,
funny stuff for all of us
sightless soul, not me.

*

Love at large
funny as it sounds,
give fruit in its season
then loves' always 'round.

If you hate the planet dirty
then it's not okay,
to take her for granted
do your part and say

"I am duty bound
'cause I'm soft on key,
just a duty to be done
for humanity."

*

The Sun came up today
let me tell you how,
I clock myself to do my best
then throw in the towel.

Up is down, yes is no ~ give it nothingness
in the soul.
Give it breath come alive. Give it 'two', see it die.
I am One of the told.

*

No entryway please
I have a rhyme,
to do the best
and never chime

without Oneness aboard
I get restless, you see
so get the best
from the touch of its chi.

*

I knew me
as the Sun yesterday,
I lost the One
to gray.

I gave it light
warm and bright,
I had a chance
to play.

*

Do the math
of none or all,
be the One
Sun from fall

love the One
in a circle of light,
be a circle.
Cause delight.

Brim and stone and fire
are One in light of me,
to cause a dark tone to light.
It's simply melody.

I write a simple sonnet
some say rough and not,
give it plenty love within
words come to the tot.

Magic has a simple sound
rough edges are not glee,
see a line move from its center
notice you and me.

Together the line
moves 'round the Sun,
plenty of time
to One.

*

I want to run up and down the mountain
and yell my name is glee,
but the residents would call authority of might
and unbeknownst to me

the people would all look puzzled
and call a cop or three,
and save the day from dark to dusk
from untold melody.

I like nature
don't keep me from me,
I'm light and woods, fish and cod
I like the day to breeze

warm light
not dark,
who took the Sun?
Could it be man's bark?

Next time you talk to a person in a vest
let them talk, don't wonder
if the love is bright, might and right.
Don't cause another blunder.

Don't take any wooden nickels
or bite that hand that feeds,
but give to the many
so there remain no needs.

Don't you catch a star by the hands?
Can a sonnet breathe like me?
Do I need to produce the One as true?
Can I buy a trusted thief?

Don't sing, let me hum
lah lah dee, dim dweedle-dee,
don't talk, let me whisper
of love and life on key.

*

Come here, talk to the wind
it answers if you listen closely,
I have a secret to tell of kings and kites
don't talk, let the breeze be me.

I am the breeze, the wind on a flow
I hither and thither and rumble and roll,
I swirl and curve and turn and blow
I whoosh and polish a sunbeam's glow.

I cry when I'm sad
I laugh when in glee,
I'm deep, I'm the ocean
come wave with me

to clouds and boats
and seals and whales,
to moonbeams and sunlight
on guessing gales.

*

"Who blew me?" I wonder.
Why guess a kite,
so still in the wind
on a moon-kissed bright night

of blustering winds wrong and right
I need to sing on key,
since the wind is all of us
and not just only me.

*

I see life in a whole new light
no muscle and brain can hold me tight,
I seize the day with all my might
I love the Light, I squeeze it tight.

By being me
and never another,
I stay myself
my soul never wanders

from he that does
me right,
not once in a while but
like morning's bright light.

More like
a mighty wind,
of a
soul soarful kite.

Let me announce
the first part of noon,
One is alone
the other's the tune.

Give it breath
watch it fly,
give it love
I'll never die

nor tomorrow or ever
so don't worry please,
the lord knows our hearts
and likes to tease

'cause we're here to stay.
"Tease what?" you may wonder.
Of life and death,
and brilliant thunder!

When you need warmth
watch Yah hey wah,
not for a thrill
but for behavior

of mercy and plea
watch me and a tree,
we both like to play
not worked 'til dis-eased.

*

Give me a break
I'll run it silly,
like a puddle of mud
I'll brim with lily.

Realistic and alone and wee
daybreak cone electricity,
never turn. Always to glee
loved from above, copy-cat me.

Never saw the lord so near
give me life like crystal clear,
duel me and break me in two
love me, you duel but on cue.

Who loves to love?
Who wants to war?
Who needs love
to the core?

I do! I need a break!
To love a soul, never take.
Give, give, give 'til it hurts,
give again, then give it a break.

Love a soul,
love me right!
Love me up,
hug me tight!

Love is a moment of two of us.
No me, just you and someone free.
Give me love and majesty,
give me someone to please.

I like to give and take with glee
I like the moment and melody,
of both the silent and the noise.
I like the day of busy boys.

Sorry girls, the boys are One
I like to fight them just for fun,

and bring them to their knees and bite
and save the day with a windy kite!

Love me as a button loose
see me as a key for two,
take me to your highest height!
Heaven abode never eschew.

*

Sonnet bear
of lovelorn care,
save me!
Help me, please!

I've been away
from the lord,
I'm down here
on my knees!

Gave a hand
up I jumped,
a kiss goes
to the One

who saved the world
environment too,
girl world one
of One.

Girl whirl
of One,
twisty twirly
knees.
Flight soar of comfort,
return of
Christ, indeed!

A sanctified must
a soul seer sound,
I gave it My name
to make it round.

Who bit the apple,
Adam or Eve?
I saw two
go to its knees.

Who wants the ending?
I do! I do!
I saw the same thing
beyond relevant you.

Why recant the past
can't change a thing,
I saw the whole you
let me show you how to sing.

A candle in the wind
a sonnet bear sound,
same One in eternity
but not a round.

A round is soft and fluffy
'cause its girly soft,
not like stones or broken bones
it's not a hard recourse.

*

Girls get the glory
tea time now for me,
if he doesn't like the rules
let man stay on bent knee.

Come soar with us, see clouds and such.
What a sight to see!
The lord has a plan for us,
be nice, don't cut a tree.

Restore the earth, plant flowers for once.
See girls live out their dream!
A lovely forest has no life,
without a happy team.

Love it as One, you are the forest.
Not so dumb after all.
The end is new. No end at all,
infinity comes in a crawl.

*

I saw a kite on Ellis Island
it reframed from being seen,
but I saw it was a spirit
of yellow blue red and green.

I see them true the spirit and me
breath of Its essence in flight,
'cause of its sound in prison dark
not me... I'm like for like.

I'm free on a breeze
I'm gone in the wind,
galloping gust
if and when

I speak loud and clear
sounds of honey,
dew breath of soul
content without money.

*

We breathe as One
and soul for fun,
I half The One
in a 50 to none

going down is
up to me,
I saw the lord
bend a tree

in a gale of breeze
to move a might,
to seer a breeze
to fly His kite.

I went to the store bought honey and pi, π.
Which is true, less or the more?
Treasures of Oneness or minds of thought
or soulful kites on a soar?

Heaven knows I'm done and through
time wise, that is...
maybe life has a rhyme to make up this time
to leave us all in a dizz.

No one breaks
my heart ever again,
I gave it to
my soul as a friend.

So never say
wait 'til tomorrow to be,
'cause waiting is stillness
contracted in me.

*

I hate depression
and winds of change,
and marketable rates
that know no end…

but I give them a 'yes'
in mercy and plea,
or my kite stays in knots
not worthy of me.

'Yes' helps me stay away from my complaining self
suffer not least I fall,
from grace from my master from above.
He loved me, I came when He called.

There's no worry in One
it's all been for fun. I love you just as you are,
in meadows and shades of glistening mirth.
Beam brightly, this shiny-bright star!

I have a friend who takes love for granted
but wants to be like me.
I said, "Softly whisper kind words of wisdom,
then love you'll always see!"

*

Return of the One is fun
if given a chance to be.
How can my mind cloud my thoughts?
Synenergy's cloudy but free.

*

Overburdened mind never gave a thought
to loosen itself from its grasp,
thinking is wearisome to the soul
like burning corn for gas.

I like my air clean and shiny
like ribbons on a bow,
I like a decorated life
of high's without the low

as circumstance would have it
I need not look around,
I have a core soar bonnet
of love too loud to sound.

Whisperless key is nothing more
but food for the soul,
because the love of innocence
is rarely ever told.

Toothless fairies know more than I
the way of the kite,
love the up and a down
to get it finally right.

*

I have that friend now
so go away, please.
The lord found me
home on my knees.

I can't get up
I'm weary and blue,
I saved myself for once
the lord was me, who knew?

Inside never fades
I like the new me,
now I give myself hugs.
Who wants to be me?

Syntax of my soul
you gave me me again!
I'm going away to find
my soul in youth, now bend

of love and light
with mercy plea,
to come of another
and not know me

is too much for the mind
I have dome for another,
to love the self
is to love a brother

who needs love and compassion
but knows not where,
to find a good friend.
The wind blows her...here!

Come get a friend
though different from me,
I need a kind
like Moses to sea.

*

I love the lord
so he loves me,
I sit real close
like a child on His knee.

He tells me everything
I know what everyone knows,
just ask Erika and Denise
they know how the wind blows.

I scare them sometimes with intimate details
of family and foe alike,
I gain when I lose touch with my friends
'cause now I'm like for like.

They look and seek and find me not
I'm written in a clue,
where muscle and brain can scare me not
'cause my lord's within me this time in my life. Who knew?

Not me! Though I'm beside myself
in red green yellow and snow,
cold winds come calling when I'm in a knot.
The lord unties my 'no'!

X-ray vision not magic or guesswork.
Come get the mike.
Can you sing on key or copy-cat me?
Be nice then, do not fight.

I'm a saint from mercy's seat
the maker meet me in you.
You know the throne of kindness, now.
I threw myself a clue.

*

I'm not too cheerful to
dance with glee,
or be in the moment
monkey knows me.

Having fun is not a lesson
it's in a moment of glee,
to turn the cheek a barrel of fun,
least we're down on one knee.

*

A sonnet is poetry
about a dream or two,
half is not the whole of it
I wish you had a clue.

It has a high voice
I thought you heard and knew,
but since the dummy couldn't hear
it came in as a clue.

Clue me
you do me right,
love has its buddy
in wrong and right

as One without the other
is lost, you see.
Both exist for the other.
Unbeknownst, it's harmony

when One is 'two'.
So, blew myself a clue
that in One there's peace,
as 'two' will erase you

from the face of man.
Then come with us, please
to harmony us again
with hug and with squeeze.

*

A moonbeam of bright light
likes to shine at night,
a dark mood's okay with us
'cause we're your guide to Light.

Want a friend in your darkest hour?
You have the lord and me,
he did His hour on a stake…
besides wrote poetry.

Round the bend I go
over open sea and more,
I love this sightless seeing.
Love driven amore.

*

Skate turn twist fall
get up on one knee,
the breeze as King of kings.
Know what the world is, please.

A kind place shows no fear
about the love loss. Turns not black,
but keeps intact a good hand-fall
on how to keep my back!

*

Eyes that twinkle in the night
look up, those are my eyes,
I see in multiplicity
I see in One disguised.

Omni is delusion
there's only One of us,
we see in multi-vision
no love, least in disgust.

Not duplicity
a One of up and down,
No. Yes. Without 'no'
no war in peaceful sound.

Love is multi-talented
has many facets, dear
of love, war and lost
and murky crystal-clear.

*

If the grass grew slower
I would admire
our lord for being free

even a dust mite
honors her kite,
be content to
be.

Be of One

Be quiet, angel of life
it's sound without end,
love this as a gift of One
a sound is better than

life as less is more of Me
not like man, I know.
I see a dying ember
before it loses glow.

Who tells from the start
the end crystal clear?
My seer has a sonnet, keen.
Who has a listening ear?

She has a take
of Me and her together,
Listen once 'cause not again,
she'll whisper it like thunder!

Her earth is done
so sad and blue,
I like the mystery
not having a clue.

A mystery
so deep in love with me,
so Christ came down
off a tree

to resurrect
a world in kind,
to tow a deed
of wondrous mind.

I flew on wings
of earth and sound,
lay not your heart
back on the ground.

Fly up here
where the air is clear,
I listen not
to stories of despair.

I freed her and Tolle
from a hopeless state,

to beam bright smiles
from all who take

life's water free
from her and Me.
Add Tolle's love,
that makes us three.

*

Breeze buzz soar
like a mighty kite,
love this life of love until
the lord is One in like.

*

Tolle likes the lord above
though he never mentioned Me,
he likes the cross of lovelorn loss
least peace he'd never see.

Heart and soul ~ guts and glory,
never be without peace.
How come the One of mercy's pride
begins in life's brief sheaf?

Lost is a perspective
of One in right,
not in 'two'
satsung sight.

*

When love's
losses grow,
big and
burdensome know

the lord is One
with us in sorrow,
tears of Now
laughs tomorrow.

"Not so big!"
said I in glee.
"I came up from
my burdened knee

of right and wrong
and misery."
So let's start anew
from scratched knees

and start humanity
with hugs and squeeze,
for you and me and
everybody sees

right and wrong
first last,
left right
never ask

in out
up down
win lose,
it's a round.

Sacred as
can be,
a circle
of humanity

sacred trusted
loved in jest,

lovelorn loss
in heaven's bliss

not up or down
or in and out,
but just One us
without the clout.

*

In One no one returns. I'm One as 'is'
no turn or stop or flee,
'cause in One it's just for fun!
Life as 'is' is Me.

A duck has his own kind of glory

Feel the power in
a motionless sea,
I feel The One breathe.
Who conquered me?

I'm a child
but not on bent knee,
I savor life whole
no part of me leaves

to take part in assembly
with mice or men,
I love the lord whole
there's nothing to mend.

I'm whole in my soul
the lord loves me as a tot,
not like twinkles in stars
'cause my kite has a 'knot'.

I'm bad sometimes
Who cares? He.
Still gave me His name.
So, I'm down from the tree.

Life is a round hole
whole with a nut,
knots are fine, too
'cause I get into ruts

like twine of night
be free on a breeze,
don't covet a woman
not on her knees.

Coveting is wrong, true
but who cares?
I'm lovelier than mice
and glorify bears.

Bears have a right
to be free on the ground,
I do too
when man's not around.

Bees buzz and hum
and so do kites,
I like the lord
He made starry-nights

that glisten and bream
and glitter and wane,
though over the moon
it crest not in vain.

The air is my friend
so is wind tunnels,

I have plenty of girlfriends now
so Tolle's no funnel

for right or wrong
or blue or red,
'cause I'm a whole.
The lord feeds me my bread.

Right is for wrong
as 'yes' is for 'no',
I have not a question.
I know how wind blows.

Up and over
and through again,
no argument here
so this is the end.

No more words out of me
'cause I'm over and done.
Clouds have their shine
in silence, they're One.

Quiet
quiet
quiet.
The lord is soundless.
Still.

Give the place sound with
glory around,
love in a kite and bill.

A duck swims in water
we know they all do,
sweet swim of glory's lot
sweet swim of his due.

Last but not least
love flowers and men,
give love to the hopeless.
Amen, amen.

*

Omni has a friend in me
my color has no grief,
a rainbow true to itself
a sword returned in sheaf.

Human needs are different from above
angels fly on wing to their destination,
I need wing nor prayer to inhabit this place
of wingless soul soar constellation.

*

Some like Me
some not,
most like it cold.
I like it hot

'cause a girl is a lair of wisdom
and a boy sings in disgust,
of love and truth and wisdom, too
he needs a lot from us.

The Maker is us
in a rock, in a tree,
come tour with Us
ride a Milky Way sea!

Love has flight
I soar on a sea,
of motionless love
I'm infinity.

*

Comfort one
comfort another
don't talk
be like thunder.

Move in One
not in three.
Sonnet of us, cognate
be.

Smart is dumb
One is us,
glorify Maker
not brawn or guts.

A girl tuned to Us
above flight,
nothingness, weariless
groan not in might.

*

Comfort of One tuned to a comet
illustrious soul, One filled with girth.
Trial of none come hither up here,
girl not of doom earns her worth.

Tell it like IT is, Oneness of freedom
life in a dream not hurried in pace,
get wisdom not doom. Alluring , yet free
glorified sadness erase.

*

Morning dove is awake in love
I love my key in love,
the Maker has a plan for us
to wear it like a glove.

Michael Jackson knew the glow within
I glow without instead,
if first I leave my soul unattended
by the lord above my head.

Lessons learn easily
in love and hate are free.
Lessons learned bought and sold
can bring me to my knees.

Glittery glove of One not 'two'
has brightness still and please,
like songs and rhymes and love and stuff
within a whirl of ease.

Round and round and round again
life without end can burn,
like embers to a flickering bee
like for like is sombered learned.

Go away clean
come back a mess,
common sense
at its best.

Matrix me

Matrix is the key
write in wind and sound,
get the best from nature's wear
come up off that ground.

You're weightless, too
remember helium's lighter than air.
I write in conundrum, sightless sight
floatless like cloud blown air.

I gave her riddle
to write about Us,
she gave milk and honey
from dustbowl to dusk.

In rhythm and rhyme
I love this place,
has mercy and love
called human race.

I'm blue sometimes
patience I adore,
it's like a swinging movement
hit flat to the floor!

Victory is sweet
when done right, a tweet
a bird tune, sung melody
lovelorn brought on beat.

Shoot it or be nor for night

A kite knows no bounds
a ear hears clearly still,
I know of love and hate now
friendship, non uphill.

Who cares who wears a gun
the lord and I save face,
shoot a soul within with love
bamboo, love and grace.

*

I see three rainbows.
Your's a three.
Mine's in matrix, see?

I talk in soul
One for me.
Removed twice in a saying,
how hard can this be?

Silence is stillness
never a sound,
creepy crawl bugs
make thunderous sounds.

Whispers are worth more
than silver and gold,
be silent for once
love never is told.

It's lived with a passion
a gusto for life,
give to a friend
like Christ, not in spite.

Love flows free
like harmony in One,
so guns are useless
if you want to have fun.

Who invented them
men or mice?
Not one soul
could say

leave them
on the ground to rot,
there's peace
in their decay.

*

Thunder drums of heaven still
beat as One up there,
heaven knows of just one friend
the wind, its lovely air.

People count, clean up the air
and then you too will see,
the love of One upon your chest
as lovely as a tree.

Breathe a tree's lovely being
be a true friend, indeed
love a tree in wisdom's stance
a breathe of love's eternity.

Allow, sit. Acceptance of the Way

Keyshia Cole
sonnet crystal clear.
"Guess What?" song
ever near.

Trumpet call
due to east,
conquer fear
when he's a beast.

Mean's not nice
cheating hurts the worst,
comfort from The One above
love not in reverse.

*

I saw One as a 9.
How could that be?
Nobody knew flight,
the lord has a key…

a note heard only
by you and by me,
we know of His truth.
Now, what do we see

in songs of angels
and love so right.
I never knew One would return.

But I hear heart music
written for me,
of lessons yet unlearned.

Proof is for sissy's
I'm a girl, so flee.
You don't want to be around
the lord and me.

Mean is for bullies
I'm peaceful to the core,
I like my moment still.
It's quiet in amore.

*

A goal less tour
of melody sweet,
so tuned for One
it kept me meek,

of lust and power
and wealth and gain.
It gave me me,
I'm whole again!

Melody has a whisperless key
nowhere to go, what would I see?
Myself again in you and a breeze
so hold on tight 'cause, I got the keys!

To open rhythm and rhyme
over oceans of time.
Love me as I am, please.

I Am infinity deep
not shallow or shy,
I go with the flow
not apple a pi, π.

A whole is not deep
it's sum of a pi,
there's more in nothing.
No-thing Am I.

I fly in a circle
I see it right,
I flew on key.
Sightless sight.

I stepped back and saw
myself on a draw,
of yellow red blue

by stepping back twice
it felt like ice,
I sing on cue for you.

I, sunshine

Daughter, I love you
feel my breath,
since a night crawler
knows no death.

Better safe than sorry
to like the One Sun,
beaver adores her
wisdom of One.

Talk to the fire
it's soft to admire,
a key of wonder
of sonnet desire.

Admire her cord
a cord of desire,
freeze on the seas
angelic guider.

*

To talk to the moon is a friend indeed
befriend a Milky Way sonnet,
the Milky Way is a place that takes its time,
to the tune of a free soaring comet.

*

Oxymoron
oxymoron,
oxymoron
not

there's more 'yes'
in a not,

more love
since I got

stillness as a friend.
A foe of many more,
then 'yes' has the vote
'cause love's got me amore.

Oxymoron
stillness be,
half full
wisdom's got

all the good's
'cause good's in me,
I love it all
in a dream worthy

'cause he went with the flow
and flew above again,
to make man whole
like a candy cane bend.

There's stripes and sweet too
like a sacrifice,
I love the warm glue
of his friendship, don't you?

Bound in friendship
though I'm not always good,
but I try with a vengeance
though there's others that should

comfort humanity with smile and glee
not like fake use of the tongue,
to talk of wisdom is good to the 't'
but more like 'yes' in the young.

Planted in a seed of grace

I have an apple tree
to swing from now.
I planted a seed of grace.

I took the high road
to work the good work
to help the human race.

Maybe my Sun doesn't shine so great
when all is said and done,
but when the wind blows of honey and grace
don't give a mind to who won the race

because skin and bones
are not of my kind,
I live in amore
and chew sunshine.

In a mountain of love
I live and breathe,
go ask the rock
it sings me, "Please,

may I go with you
to know grace and love?"
because my rock
has no love.

Two of a kind
my rock and me,
I need the Sun
my rock needs me.

We know each other
like mercy and plea,
and sing in One.
Diphthong key

'cause we're weary and tired
in need of love,
'cause the moon has a caste
and our Sun's made of love.

Different is good at times, you see
but when it hurts to be different from me,
then just be patient and kind and true
'cause god's got his heart fixed solely on you.

*

No amount of money will please a man.
Why not be free?
A tree has shade and fruit and stuff,
money has no leaves.

Give money to a poor man
he needs his daily bread,
to get a meal in patience.
It's good when all are fed.

Poor and needy are One being
of light and love and just,
give and take gives to One.
Giving is a must.

*

Chest full of
wire and sound,
rowboat of kite
wear to the ground,

on a motionless beach
I cried a soft sigh,
to beam god's mercy
a breeze tour toward sky.

*

Masterpiece theater in a song
I wrote myself in time,
to get a loose from binded knee.
Too fruitful to be blind.

I like the lord in a tree
of yellow leaves come fall,
softly falling to the ground
'neath blue skies or not at all.

'Cause like a bird in flight on wings of might
in seldom need of money,
I get a wish of sonnet sound
bee balm tone comb honey.

*

I was good to many
didn't have a clue,
I knew not of The One
I knew only 'two'.

Sorry if I hurt you
forgive me please you see,
I like myself not in a knot
I like me good and free.

*

I saw my Sun
cry in denial,
but gave it a sonnet
to clear away sorrow.

I saw the blue sky
tricky and blue,
the sky is a trick
of comic gloom.

I need my space
to write of we,
to save a soul
to give a plea.

Nice to be back
and come of love,
to tour alone
to wear a glove

of new and old
and love and hate.
To be bold and say,
"I ate the cake."

I gave it away
to talk of love,
to bring in hope
from god above.

I love my job
and never hate,
to write a sonnet
to close a gate.

To make it clear
and cloudy still,
but my love for god
is better ill

then to talk
of fame or money as though,

to give a job of
kind and hope

to get some time
to evaluate,
the situation
of love not hate.

Give me room to breathe
give me love and hope,
give me milk and honey
got my god to cope.

I like to write of love
sold nothing to be here,
I love to come and go
and hear a sound so dear

as "Please be with
the lord and me,
and come up off
that bent knee!"

Because the love of
man is huge,
because god has love
yet unused.

*

Wisdom the sky
leave no work undone,
leave a place of misery
to run and go have fun!

*

Bee breeze of sweet sound
known to the ground,
a waterless cavern knows its depth
a moonbeam knows its sound.

It makes butterfly flutters
and flashes of light,
and breams with love
and delight in flight.

*

A person of One
to take the reign,
to give love a change
of power and range.

I know love has a memory
of sweet love and song,
to sing in the wind
how nothing went wrong.

The day is gifted
even in snow, rain and sleet.
Let me lift your soul up
because you didn't sleep.

Awareness in One helps a bit
when weary and tired to the bone.
Give gift of life to the weary this time.
Give love to those loving god's throne.

I can't give
money or things,
I'm not a worker
of magic

yet I give love and trust
and time to those,
who thought it was love
that was tragic.

To know the lord
would come to me,
and help me but a child

a gifted life I have by his side
for eternity now,
'cause love for his cause I won't hide.

He gave his key ~ I use it at will
I love my life on pi, π
'cause I'm liked by millions and billions, too.
They like his kite, so do I.

Wind chill factor to equal Sun's sum

π (*pi*) rated
but cool to the touch,
don't know the sum of Sun
'til core briefed in noon, as such.

*

Tango on the tight rope of desire
befell the common man,
soared beyond belief
to a distant foreign land.

One Sun gloomy and blue
save it for tomorrow.
Bee wax of honey can be funny
even in its sorrow.

Cognate sea in love with the soul
come with us, a must
to glory and winds unbounded
by body's downward dust.

*

Save the planet
is a crux due to plea,
basil at dusk
abreast on a breeze.

*

To befriend a cloud
is One of its kind,
to be of this
is to free up the mind.

*

I fly in the sky to water the bird
to give free is where,
tour in denial, speak speech of One
cantaloupe be pear.

*

Unmatched by pride or tide
but free to soar,
ageless mind wanderer
can close a door.

Dawn an early night
crickets like me, still.
Bees don't fly back when honey's full
they walk back to the till.

*

I get a chewer to talk about
when we save a nation,
from going down
a road of destruction.

I see a good twist
I manifold,
aware of my power
juxtaposed.

To gift a child
of mercy and plea,
and gain a trust
of wind over sea.

*

I got to have it quiet
least I'm sad and blue,
closed minds are loud and cloudy.
Shush the person next to you.

Bee fly to tour
away to throne,
cottage a noon
bear to roam.

If I mistletoe again
stay right here,
comfort tour started
on cloud floating air.

Twilight

I like the Sun, it is within me.
As the moon I shine within, too
but in the end when the sun and moon ellipse
I can too be of their due.

Why is the world round, sound and at ease?
Where humanity of its 'One'?
Rest, be free of this one-sided life
love the moon, come Sun!

Breathless touch, moonless soulful soar.
Where the brave among us as One with love?
Given to a bushel of two.
Lessen a grip on love when it's above

given to two. Lessen it as dove, then.
As One of a kind least two be brave kin.
Wisdom is of its source in love above.
Kind flyer above as in space when chagrin

of One which is No-thingness or bust.
Flyer of the wind, I AM.
Keeper of humanity 'til naught.
Done now, if not then when?

*

See forward
wavy mind tone,
lei world full of love
kind mind clone.

*

Captain steers for shore
to break a mighty wave,
to keen its awareness
bats of One can save.

*

Memory daunted
away from the curl,
wavy ring
contented whirl.

*

Can bring about order
touch the sky,
infinity deep
never deny.

*

I have a Father, too. Of course you only knew
of One of us not the other.
To give of love and not of hate
is the glove of love another.

Too course the gear be a wearer,
of pink petals not blue.
I saw a melody of grace and tone
so great her flower grew.

*

Give it a clue to follow
save it for tomorrow.
Wednesday is gone, Tuesday is free.
sonnet sound of sorrow.

Keeper of the hearth

Tour core rhyme reason
needs a place to see,
One in a crowd of infinite
sees borne in me

per talent core of justice
sleuth cometh dawned in dusk.
Save this place unchord by reason
preserving thrust through dust.

Unburdened in the womb of want
desirous of nothing be.
Comforted beyond these baronless tides of grief.
'Yes' is the answer in me.

'No' is not worthy.
Let go of no, desist.
No more wanderer of girth nor prowl,
beneath a sector of time least

we borrow never to pay
bringing grief to its sloth.
Bereft of no one, anywhere.
Infinity soothes in awe.

An unlikely woe
in need of a child in grin,
to loosen its grip of no-where's fun
loving it as a kin.

A king on a throne knows no power
like 'Yes' has in its mirth,
undoodled as a rhyme yet sung
deliriously borne of its girth.

Seethe in the girdle
seem to be sum,
of water and ice.
Sonnet is done

winged on a prayer
giving wisdom of One,
keeper of Light -
return of the Sun!

I saved the best for last
to write a sonnet keen,
seer unbroken, tightrope walker.
Instant mind redeem.

China Seas beckons us whole

Comfort is in our *Oneness of Being.*
Softly we lay down our arms of war,
so peace returns to us. Be loving, true.
Stealth midst avatar

for what truly works for love.
Wanting to win for the sake of another,
see how far away from harmony.
Begin again, love your brother

in clothed as peace beyond any star
or stellar beauty above.
We've come to do worthiness
midst its love drawn dove.

Who would stop our infinite flight
its need to call us to One?
Simple as it is to love
heaven knows some run.

Flight of a key whispered in dawn's wake
to shutter a bug or two. Twinkly star above for
love's just right. Take the hand of
another for the sake of its condor

of flight among man. Who sees air yet wind?
Breaming amidst a world in kind.
Battle not your foe. For neither friend
nor foe untwine

our Mystery when we borne ourselves whole.
Leaning forward in dust,
to return one day a mighty force
of wisdom blown as us.

Lovely is a tree come winter too.
Love will have its say, so please
assist another come rain or shine.
Come up off bent knees.

Find life new with wisdom our lot.
Hurry sir! Wisdom won in One.
Figured you want to understand, to know
why love began in *fun*!

To get away from war seems strange
to many, not just few.
How else is love to peace our stead?
Love a leaf come fall, just you.

In One peace needs you alone.
No one else need take your place.
How can anyone else be you?
You are me, human race.

Let a cloud soar come China's tune
for Lebanon's known in space,

know we come from above, mankind.
Love in us is grace.

Come June we weather bright our tune
no matter where we come to be.
Love as though we're wisdom's lot.
Whisper it on key.

Why tune a turtle to a world in kind?
We all need our space, it's true.
Comfort now on wings of glory
so we its beauty grew.

Flowering consciousness beckons.
Allow this too 'to be'.
For 'not to be' is just as One
in our soft spoken tone, a whisper*less* key.

Kite a day in Mystic One
love's a being in us all.
Too, lean toward its tongue
though *Being* comes forth in a crawl.

Wisdom of One

(...*now some people will not like this
last verse but we are slow when it comes to
being nice. There, I said it. Whew!*)

Conclusion

This is the real deal. If you read this it will change us. Whatever doesn't break us will move us. Love has taken its toll. In either direction it will work.

I wrote this book because of the dismissal of what is true in ourselves needs to be worked on a bit. I wanted to talk about love because I knew if we could all just somehow get past the hardheartedness we've seem to have gotten into the habit of playing on our daily lives that hopefully with enough heartfelt plea maybe things would change.

I am heartbroken, I sense life's sadness too much. When I told my oldest daughter I was writing a book to help people relax and to look to the truth of our being that life is good, she mentioned to me to talk to people about love on the relationship-side of the issue as we all know love has many facets.

My daughter can't seem to find a mate. I said to her, "Relationships huh?" As modern Spiritual Master on The Power of Now Eckhart Tolle mentioned, our relationships are the playground where the wanton unconscious behavior of our soul likes to reside until enough foolishness with its pain and suffering would produce a spiritual awakening to be itself whole.

I didn't know what nor how to approach what seemed like a heartache in the making. To the effort of my daughter I would like to thank you all, too.

This trilogy was written so as to hopefully assist us to grow up in our duty assigned us. A good portion of humanity still lives in fear. I profusely apologize if any toes felt they we stepped on. That was never my intent.

So, all we go down the road of existence as we should. Let's see, love has a way of being. We are not 'It' yet. Well, we are...

Don't let the words assume I have the final adjusting solution, I haven't. But as I have mentioned, love is just a word if used to mask our reality that we haven't a clue who's going to get the job done.

My daughter is my business to see that she fairs well. "Not an easy task!" some will chime in for even though adult children are grown and long since have their own lives to move along with, the heartache most sense comes from 'deep within of knowing' the truth that consciousness is just in its infancy. Time and patience our weapons of choice where love improves is at our doorstep. Love is a blessed state. May your journey be light not just of consciousness but with the joy of being 'It.'

To Erika, may your children speak wisdom in due time for fruitage blossoms as consciousness would have their foliage moist, ripe and right on time. (...the other two, at least.) No one right way to be nice, true?

To Rebecca my darling daughter and hers in kind our sweet Jada ~ you two save the last dance for that someone truly worthy, for life is short and beauty your being. I love you Rebecca and remember it's family first.

To my other two, be sweet. Hopefully in time you will like what Mother has to offer, too. Money has its place (...whew!) Your Dad gave it. This time around don't misjudge that love is for losers, though. The love of my mothering are seeds of compassion and its wisdom and a softness money would harden. Don't see care or beauty except within a matchless scale of wisdom alongside of its greatest prize to be won, a heart full of love alone. You two have time for growth yet, still.

Who I'll remember most Penelope LeFaucheur of San Antonio's 'Second Chance Foundation'. You are open armed to a fault. You generously give of all your possessions, money and time wise to those in earnest need of assistance. Being reared in India, you hold a spirit to be generous and kind toward the poor of society that endears all to your soul. What a model of love, I honor your spirit. I hope to emulate your deeds of compassion.

About the book

Beauty of our societies worldwide

Can we be One at last?

As man is waking up out of his state of illusion to include even the lowliest among us, may we be blessed away from our indifference and into the waiting arms of love itself to all it matters at present. Harmony and Oneness permeates the theme so as to assist humanity to a spiritual awakening as such assistance is needed in our day and time.

Love be of One.

About the author

Anna Coffer having suffered much turmoil from experiencing what most experience today, an absence of love either from self or society including intimate family members whereas she set out to hold out to humanity the one most precious gift life has to offer, love.

Enlightenment and consciousness are just words. Beauty has a way of being. So, the ladder being our soul in its own right she sets out to discuss worldwide once and for all, *Be of One*. Wholeness of humanity is our inheritance should we break free from fear in all its disguises therefore Being of One was a great endeavor for her to undertake to express what meant love to a soul whethering to be of peace again. Let's begin then…

In fear we lose peace.

Contact the Author

E-mail

onenessofbeing@annacoffer-onenessofbeing.com

Website

www.annacoffer.com

www.annacoffer-onenessofbeing.com

A Return of the Sun

Quess what?

You're going to have to love

somebody.

The key to our growth in *consciousness* ~ bless another

There are many keepers of peace among mankind ~ be it officers of law and order through to Judges who are so overwrought to have to experience so little love coming from our societies. They too warrant peace.

Here…a book to assist.

Blessed be

Other books by the author

Spirit Seas
Sonnets of Oneness Inspired by Eckhart Tolle

You Can't Take Your Credit Card
With You When You Go…
Book 1

You Can't Take Your Credit Card
With You When You Go..
Book 2

also
Coming Soon

Tidal Wave Rider ~ Wing Over Water
plus
Universal Consciousness
Oneness of Being

Enjoy the entire series